BOLD COLORS
FOR MODERN ROOMS

ROCKPORT

GLOUCESTER MASSACHUSETTS

BOLD COLORS
FOR MODERN ROOMS

BRIGHT IDEAS FOR PEOPLE WHO LOVE COLOR

SARAH LYNCH

ROCKPORT
PUBLISHERS

First published in the United States of America by
Rockport Publishers, Inc.
33 Commercial Street
Gloucester, Massachusetts 01930-5089
Telephone: (978) 282-9590
Facsimile: (978) 283-2742
www.rockpub.com

ISBN 1-56496-807-3

10 9 8 7 6 5 4 3 2 1

Design: Otherwise, Inc.
Production and Layout: Terry Patton Rhoads
Cover Image: Picture Press

Printed in China.

INTRODUCTION

Color is one of the trickiest elements of interior design to master. Who doesn't worry in the face of a seemingly infinite array of paint chips and fabric swatches? And now with advanced dyeing techniques making it possible to color almost any material, even the simple practice of buying a blender becomes an exercise in color matching—should you pick cobalt blue or cherry red to go with your bright yellow kitchen? Take a moment to notice how often color weaves through our lives and you will see bold, bright color on everything from lawn chairs to electronics, velvet to stainless steel, and kitchens to cars. And if you're like me, you are both overjoyed at the prospect of throwing out all the putty gray and sage green in favor of a more daring palette, yet slightly intimidated by the endless possibilities of wild color combinations.

Although vibrant colors may arrive with a reputation leaning toward tacky, a carefully considered brilliant palette can be tremendous. This book was written to offer you the tools and advice you need for choosing bold colors, and also to give you inspiration—and the courage to make color your own. Sure, the just-right mix of vibrant yellow with acid green can be a delicate balance, but pairing a neutral with "natural" is hardly an accomplishment. Decorating with bold colors is like cooking with exotic spices—it takes some exploration to find the blend you like. In these pages, you'll find red hot color recipes designed to challenge and entice you to make color your style signature.

Once you are ready to parallel your personality with brights, complement your collections with wilds, or match your moods with mods—it is a good idea to consider exactly what you want your colors to say before going out and buying gallons of paint. Vivid color gets attention, and this book offers a central piece of advice: Color is a personal style choice and no one can tell you which colors are right and which are wrong. If red makes you feel strong and flaming orange gives you a kick, it doesn't much matter that these colors may make your room feel a tiny bit smaller. These are bold colors for modern rooms.

HOW TO USE THIS BOOK

This is not a how-to book—simply because there is no step-by-step recipe to color success. Color is not a standardized concept in the same way that furniture styles and design movements can be. Instead, color reflects a state of mind; it is an ancient and abstract path to personal expression and style. Bright, vibrant colors are universal, energizing, and vital. People who choose to live among such vivid hues and intense colors are not the kind to follow recipes, anyway. In the pages that follow, you will find beautiful photographs, some practical advice, a few interesting facts, and lots of encouragement. This is an idea book intended to lead you into the world of bold color and let you discover your own colorful way.

Of the eight chapters that follow, six are dedicated to each of the major hues. The final two chapters address practical issues, including ways to create multi-colored palettes and fast fixes for minor color mishaps. These chapter divisions are by no means exclusive; if you have your heart set on using green, you can start there, but be sure to explore some of the other possibilities because you will find plenty of green in Cool Blues. Red pops up frequently in the Shocking Pinks and Purples chapter and there is orange throughout Bold Yellows. And don't forget to check out Mix It Up for some color combining lessons that will inspire you to mix any combo from two to seven colors in your palette.

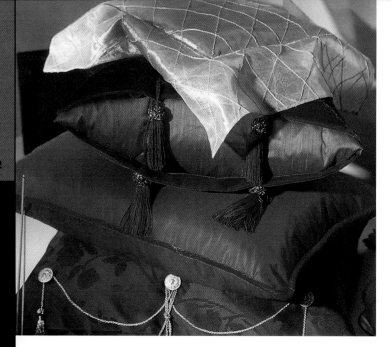

The chapters on the primary colors—red, yellow, and blue—are loosely organized by room. These three colors have the most universal affects on people and have been widely researched for use in the home; thus there are some rooms where a cool blue works beautifully for the purposes of that space and other places where yellow might be just what is needed. The chapters on secondary colors—orange, purple/pink, and green—are given a little more room to explore the range of shades they cover. These chapters offer a sampler of ideas for the more protean colors that shift from one primary to another. For instance, the chapter on orange begins with a selection of yellow-orange and ends with deeper shades of red-orange. And since there are more varieties of green than any other color—from turquoise to kelly green to lime green—each is bold enough to be included in order to cover as many brights as possible. The chapter on purple/pink sways a little between these two colors that borrow from both red and blue and the result is a far-reaching range that is both daring and soft.

The last chapter, Fast Fixes, is a good place to start if you have a specific color problem. This chapter is divided into major color problems that many of us run into when faced with bright hues and lots of them: From what to do if your color isn't bright enough, is too bright, or is simply not at all what you expected.

Fast Fixes also offers solutions for moderating strong color that has taken over a room by making it feel too hot, too small, or too sweet. The practical advice gives lessons in using accents, complementary colors, paint techniques, and lighting solutions to keep color fresh and bold.

Finally, since color trends come and go, we hope you'll turn to this volume again and again, as you would to a friend: there is always room for fresh inspiration because the greatest thing about color is that it doesn't have to be expensive or permanent.

BOLD YELLOWS

The fastest way to energize any space that feels dull or tired is to use a high-voltage yellow. A bright yellow kitchen turns up the heat for high-energy cooking. Furnishings in the boldest yellows add an instant dash of zest to a dining room. Living rooms and outdoor spaces that cry out for a healthy dose of vibrant color can be easily treated with a gallon of lemon-yellow paint on the walls, trim, furniture, or even the ceiling.

If you are looking for a cheerful atmosphere, don't be afraid to go for the gold. Keep in mind that bright yellow, the color of sunshine, will naturally go with everything, so don't hold back. Let the ubiquitous quality of yellow be your encouragement to use it liberally. Once confined to the kitchen or used in the form of a whispery pastel for baby's nursery, bold and bright yellows are now popping up everywhere. In fact, the popularity of yellow has even gone beyond the modern design classics of Alessi kitchen accessories and Herman Miller furnishings. This primary hue can now be found in nearly every incarnation from contemporary furnishings to new electronics and appliances ranging from stereos to mixers.

Yellow's sunny associations will work hard to impart a sense of warmth and good cheer wherever it is used so don't be concerned about toning down the brightness or muddying the vibrancy. Yellow is meant to be fun, cheerful, and youthful. Take advantage of these properties by using it in places where this excitement is needed. Plain vanilla hallways will seem more like a tunnel of light if enveloped, floor-to-ceiling, in a luminous shade of yellow. And yellow can be the missing inspiration for a home office or study, even when used as an accent on a single wall or bookshelf.

↑
White with any color, but particularly yellow, will bring out the freshness and truth of the color.

↖
Yellow is the only color that cannot be darkened, the more saturated it becomes, the brighter and more vibrant it appears.

The best places to use yellow are rooms where more energy is desired. It is not the best color for relaxation or meditative places where cooler shades like bold blues and clean greens might work better than an attention-getting yellow. Instead, use this sunny color to banish the blahs from active spaces such as your dressing area, a breakfast nook, and even the garage.

← A galvanized hanging wall file against a yellow and purple background equals serious business. The pair of complementary colors makes them each stand out and the surface of the metal shines for an eye-catching corner that will beckon you to check your in-box. Try employing a similar tactic for that dark corner where the mail always piles up before you notice.

← In entrances and on front doors, impart a feeling of welcome. Start with bright, primary yellow on the door, but don't stop there. A daring yellow entryway makes for a memorable entrance.

FACT FILE:

1. YELLOW IS THE MOST EYE-CATCHING COLOR; USE IT ANYWHERE YOU WANT TO DRAW ATTENTION.

2. YELLOW AND BLACK IS THE BOLDEST COLOR COMBINATION, BE CAREFUL USING THEM TOGETHER FOR GRAPHIC STRENGTH: THINK OF A BUMBLEBEE OR A YIELD SIGN.

3. PURPLE IS YELLOW'S COMPLEMENT; PAIR THEM TOGETHER FOR A DRAMATIC EFFECT.

4. YELLOW IS THE ONLY COLOR THAT CANNOT BE DARKENED, THE MORE SATURATED IT BECOMES, THE BRIGHTER AND MORE VIBRANT IT APPEARS.

5. YELLOW IS SAID TO PROMOTE MENTAL CLARITY AND IMPROVE CONCENTRATION: SO USE IT LIBERALLY IN A HOME OFFICE.

→ For darker or less than inspirational settings, color is of the greatest importance. For this home office under a staircase, a jolt of lemon yellow on the wall may be the only source of inspiration. Take advantage of the benefits of bold colors when designing a home office—yellow can lift your mood and make work seem like play. According to color therapists, the yellow on the walls will make for smarter and faster work, too.

CITY SLICKER

RUBBER DUCKY

TAXI CAB

LEMON DROP

YELLOW ZEST

JUICY

DAFFODIL

SUNFLOWER

YELLOW MAKES A FLAVORFUL KITCHEN

Yellow has always been a kitchen classic, resurfacing as stylish again and again. When deciding on colors for a kitchen, go ahead and use the boldest, brightest yellows that you want, but make sure the palette is appetizing. This doesn't have to mean weak or pale. Instead, consider tangy citrus, tart sorbet, and even glossy jellybean hues. Follow your instincts, remembering to handle yellow greens with extra care (so they won't feel acidic) and mustard yellows with a watchful eye (lest they turn muddy or gray).

The color recipes you choose will also help to determine the overall palette and theme of the room. Choose accents and combinations inspired by the delicious: strawberry red with bright banana; lemon with lime and tangerine; or soft yellow and tart grapefruit-pink.

Color is essential for kitchens and bold, daring yellows work particularly well because they add a much-needed jolt to what is often a standard setting. Unlike other rooms in the home (which are filled with furniture and collectibles) kitchens are filled with necessities first: design options may be limited once such essentials as refrigerators, ranges, dishwashers, and sinks are in place. Luckily, yellow is great with all the standard-issue materials; reflecting beautifully in stainless steel counters, warming to the cold industrial feel of appliances, and looking fresh and bright against white enamel fixtures.

↑
A mixture for a tangy margarita—zesty lemon, orange, and grapefruit come together for a zesty tiled kitchen.

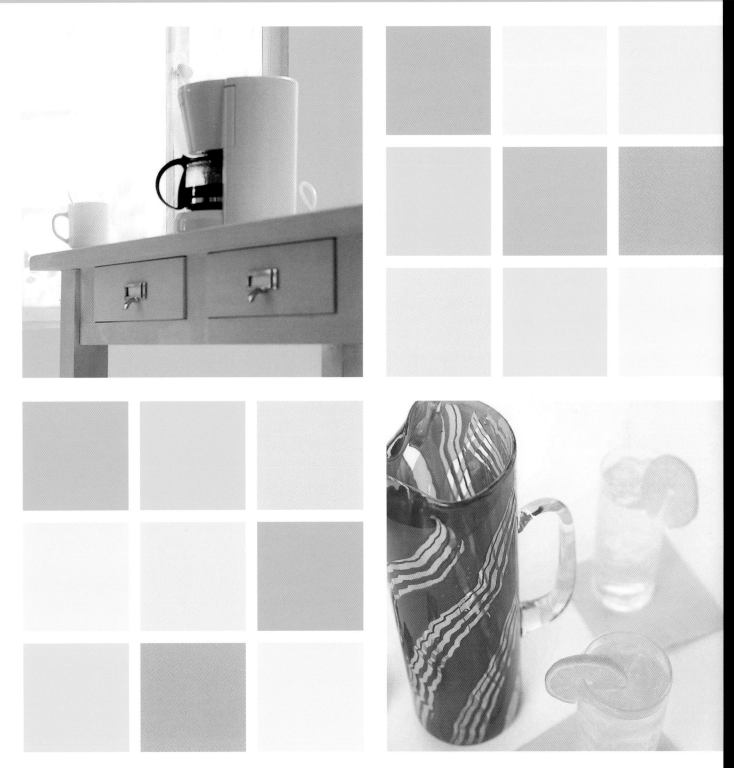

COLOR HARMONY WITH YELLOW

The effect of a monochromatic yellow color scheme can be a relief, but it can also be overwhelming, particularly if it is not balanced with a variety of textures and tones. In this case, harmonious color combinations will work just as well to keep a room looking organized. Match yellow with a neighboring color such as orange or green, but be sure to use them in equal intensities. A powerful yellow will wilt a pale green and make a peachy orange look plain silly. Mix adjacent colors in equal portions and equal strengths for the boldest effect. Designers frequently use harmonious color combinations as a way to make colors more livable without toning them down. For instance, if you want to use yellow but want it to be a very warm yellow, combine it with orange. For a yellow that doesn't feel too hot in an already warm climate, temper it with a cool leafy green.

↗
Lemon or lime? This seems to be the question here as both shades compete for the starring role. Although there is a greater proportion of vivid yellow, the lime green seems to pop off the cabinets. These two colors play off each other: calling out the other in contrast while reflecting their partners' tones.

→
Harlequin designs in golden yellows turn this standard living room into a space for bright ideas.

→ →
This galley kitchen appears longer and more modern with a bright yellow wall as a focal point; the hanging yellow lampshades draw attention as well. When using yellow, remember that it makes objects jump to the forefront: the viewer will see anything in yellow first.

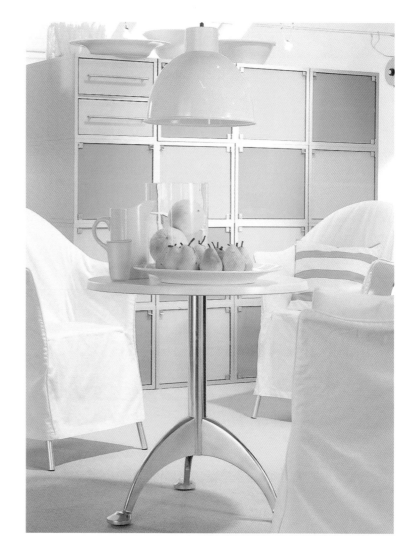

YELLOW PLUS WHITE MAKES SPACE AND HEIGHT

If strong pairs of color (yellow plus red) seem overwhelming in a small room, try matching yellow with bright white. White with any color, but particularly yellow, will bring out the freshness and truth of the color. Many designers like to emphasize a single vibrant hue against a background of non-colors—like white, black and gray—in order to fool the eye. In the kitchen a brilliant yellow wall at one end can become a focal point, drawing attention to make the room appear longer and larger. Yellow may then be woven in as an accent to emphasize the warmth of polished wood floors or cabinetry.

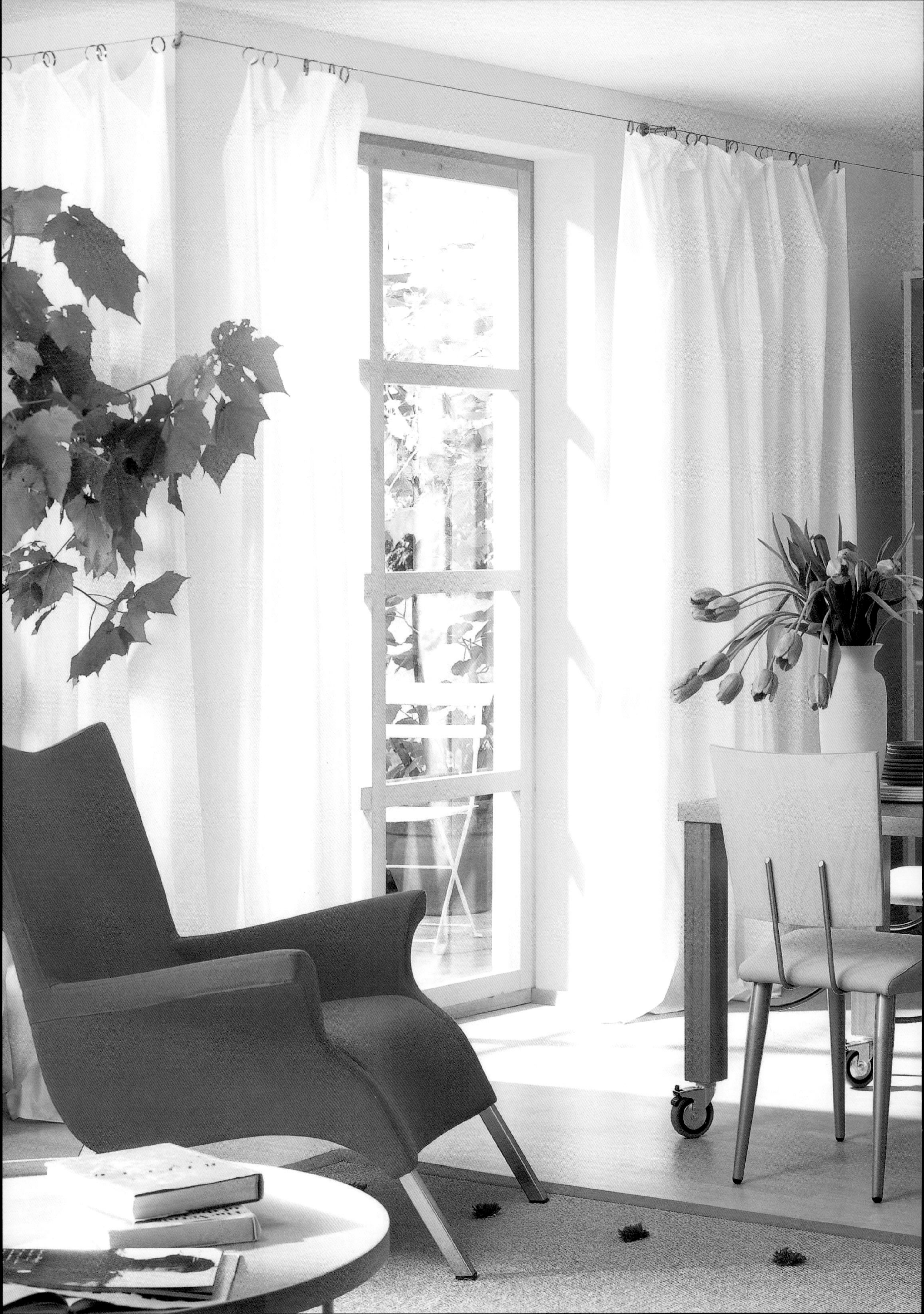

YELLOW LOVES DINING ROOMS

Vibrant yellows are a great choice for dining areas for many of the same reasons that they work so well in the kitchen: they promote a good mood and cheery conversation while the flavorful shades rev up the appetite. In more formal dining rooms, the effect of an all-yellow wash lit by candlelight leaves a glowing memory. For areas that get very little sunlight, using bright yellow as a substitute light source is the perfect remedy. In many homes, dining rooms are situated as a walk-through area off of a kitchen or living room, leaving them feeling cold with almost no exposure to light. The easiest and cheapest way to cozy up a dreary, windowless dining area is to add a warm coat of yellow paint. The presence of vibrant color will be a surprise where we would normally expect classic sages and formal slate blues.

Designers lament that dining rooms, which are normally the most carefully designed areas in the home, are used only on special occasions. All design efforts are wasted if the end result is a fussy and formal "dining room" rather than a comfortable modern eating area for family and friends to gather. In fact, many designers are doing away with the notion of a space reserved exclusively for dining, keeping in mind that most people now use these areas less for entertaining than as a multi-purpose area for eating, working, and doing homework. In this case, high-energy colors like yellow, orange, and pink work harder than any neutral for a more active and less formal environment.

←
A sunny yellow on the walls of this light-filled eating area, accented with tropical splashes of bold orange, adds to a sense of summer dining. Bleached canvas window panels enhance the effect. Greenery is a natural friend of yellow, always right at home in a golden atmosphere.

For rooms blessed with giant windows and a flood of light, an electrifying yellow is a natural asset. Well-lit spaces can afford to use yellows in their most saturated hues because they can stand up to the abundance of sunlight. This kind of lighting makes it the perfect scenario to envelope an entire room in one bright color; or a great place to mix up the boldest color combinations like yellow teamed with a hot pink or flaming orange. Try accenting a slicker-yellow sofa with purple cushions in a place where the light will keep the color true, for a look that is loud but not overbearing.

Wherever you use yellow, don't forget about the evening hours when artificial lighting will make this color appear brighter and more saturated. Always keep the lighting source (for both day and evening) in mind when choosing a hue. As a rule, incandescent lights will intensify yellow, fluorescents will counter and dull it with a bluish-green cast, and halogen will keep it true to its daylight appearance.

↖
If you've invested in dark wood cabinets and marble counters for your deluxe kitchen, but find the overall result too dark and heavy, brighten things up a bit with a splash of primary yellow. Glass-topped tables and translucent furnishings can also help diminish the heft of luxe materials while adding a necessary touch of whimsy.

←
Use washed yellow ocher to create the impression of saturated sunlight and warmth. Fresh-cut flowers make this workspace seem more like a solarium than an office. Notice how the wash used on the wood paneled walls creates a more natural, vibrant effect than standard, opaque paint because it appears dappled with sunlight.

←
The best places to use yellow are rooms where more energy is desired. Bold colors are naturally uplifting and yellow, in particular, simulates the warm energy of sunlight.

BRILLIANT YELLOWS ENERGIZE

Bright yellows make us feel warmer by the sheer heat of their vibrancy and can make a room appear lighter by simulating sunlight. Depending on the depth of the yellow, it can also make a very large room appear cozier. And, it is indisputable that brilliant yellows will energize and add interest to any room. Think about these "special effects" of yellow and use them to your advantage when considering colors for your home. A room with little heat or sun exposure will radiate with a hot yellow on the walls or a fuzzy golden rug. Even cramped quarters under the eaves can become cozy and charming with the added luster of yellow and orange—especially if you can emphasize the palette by exposing wood floors. For work/live areas the brightest shades of yellow serve to turn up the volume. A multi-purpose space for modern living, this room (below, right) is for someone who works hard and plays hard. Yellow doesn't take itself too seriously, especially when paired with a candy-colored orange, so use it in places that could use a laugh or a dose of irreverence.

↗

Baths are generally meditative spaces that tend to look polished in cool aquas, or sweet purples, pinks, or peach. In design, however, no rules are firm. The dark environs of this small bath under the sharp-slanting eaves needed extra glow for warmth. Bold yellow and bright orange provide a fiery combination that heats up this bath yet still imparts a sense of calm.

→

Here, colors of a playground transform a home office and storage area into a high-energy space that feels like fun. Consider this when planning kid's spaces (even big kids) and forget the hushed pastels.

LIGHT UP A
LIVING ROOM WITH YELLOW

One of the most interesting facts about yellow is that you can't really make it darker, only paler or more vibrant. Normally the more saturated a color becomes, the deeper the effect, but yellow gets only brighter and brighter. Any attempt to darken yellow paint, by adding black or any other dark color, will muddy it and make it look either brown, green, or something awful in between. In spaces in the home reserved for public use or entertaining, this becomes the dilemma with yellow.

When decorating formal living rooms, most people tend to lean toward a more conservative palette. But for those who prefer bolder hues, yellow is an excellent option because it can match almost any style. Paint the walls in a bright canary yellow or goldenrod. The harmonious nature of bright yellow allows the color to blend with everything from chintz to bold graphics to warm wood tones.

If you are easing into bold and bright, or concerned it might be too much for entertaining, balance it out with touches of pale green or an earthy orange. Another option, of course, is to play up a high-voltage yellow by allowing it to be the singular color—the glowing star of the show. If visits from the timid are not a concern, try adding yellow fabrics that have a little bit of sheen like a solid chintz or silk blend for either upholstery or window treatments and your living room will become a luminous retreat.

Yellow, the preeminent color in nature, can be a unifying factor for even the most disparate collections. Few people are starting from scratch when they think about redecorating, and this is particularly true when it comes to living rooms. Unlike a bedroom, which can be given a facelift in a flash with a can of paint and new linens, living rooms must take into account substantial furnishings that were probably an investment and possibly heirlooms. Not only that, but living rooms are generally where the "stuff" goes: TV's and entertainment systems as well as collections and artwork meant to be displayed.

Dramatic living rooms often rely on good editing— but those who have many belongings shouldn't have to start over. Focusing on a single eye-catching color can make a room appear more organized. Think of a mis-matched collection of vintage radios or vacation postcards against a bright yellow background, the boldness of the color draws the eye and holds attention rather than competing with the collection. And even bold yellow seems to be neutral. Where red or blue might somehow change our experience with too much urgency or intent, a warm yellow shines brightly on our belongings.

→
Feel free to play all your cards at once: bright colors, bold patterns, funky details, and metallic accents come together in this room for a fearless final outcome. Black and white graphic patterns stand out boldly against a bright color such as this taxi cab yellow.

Perhaps the power of yellow seems too strong in your tiny living area, but you want to maintain the statement of this bold hue? In this case, go ahead and use black and white shapes and patterns but make sure to balance this traffic-stopping combination with some neutral elements. In the room seen here, the blazing yellow walls are accentuated by the white fireplace and upholstered chairs with graphic animal print cushions. At the same time, the color seems to be disarmed by the warm tones in the polished wood floors and coffee table. Even the gilded mirror over the mantel is offset by a decoupage screen and golden throw. This is a room of yin and yang, where black and white is balanced with mild forms and textures and a daring shade of yellow is mellowed by the honey tones in the wood. It still makes its statement but leaves room for living.

↑
Yellow goes perfectly with stainless bookshelves or brushed metal stereo equipment. Paired with a bold orange, the colors become a warm central theme, drawing focus to the smart yellow and orange design elements.

↑
The best way to show off nice curves is to set them against a dramatic background; here a scrolling plaster mantel and a pair of soft white seating stand out against blazing sunset yellow walls. The graphic effect of black and white silhouettes are translated to a reverse print that is less stark but equally bold.

→
Use yellow thoughtfully. Although it is a sunny color, it can become relentlessly optimistic. Be sure to use it only where high energy and sunshine are appropriate. This verdant oasis is the perfect spot to capture the color of sunshine.

YELLOW AND GREEN GET FRESH

Designers frequently seek inspiration outdoors when creating color schemes, because people inherently find these combinations pleasing. With this in mind, an excellent match for yellow is green. Not only is green an adjacent color, lying next to yellow on the spectrum, but it is also the hue of leaves and greenery that complement almost every yellow flower, fruit, and vegetable. Consider using this combination in any room that requires a feeling of freshness, like a kitchen or a damp basement or attic. In environments that are teeming with lushness and foliage, use yellow in its brightest capacity. The look will be as powerful as the sun pouring down on a verdant landscape. In porches or sitting areas, yellow can be played up to the highest degree with the addition of black-and-white striped cushions and a hi-gloss lacquer on the furniture.

WILD ORANGES

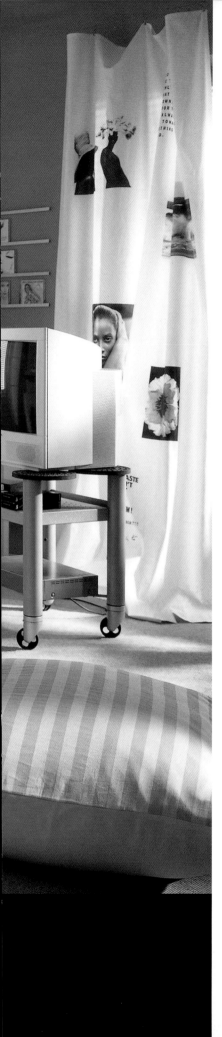

A mixture of arresting red and optimistic yellow, orange glows with warmth and positive energy. Bright orange symbolizes fun, play, active adventure, and, by all means, daring. Orange ranges from yellow-based shades on one side and red-toned oranges on the other with citrus-flavored colors in the middle. Wild and wonderful orange has vivid associations with candy, toys, and high-tech gadgets. Use it to set the stage for lighthearted living while making a strong style statement.

No matter which hue you pick, orange will always be a friendlier choice than red and a more daring decision than yellow. Without a doubt, orange is the happiest color in the spectrum. Though long reserved for children's bedrooms and playrooms, don't let that cloud your imagination. It works well for warmly lit bedrooms and sleek kitchens. Living rooms and dining areas will benefit from the radiance of this outgoing color. Opt for a candy-colored orange in any space that feels dark and dreary, and the brightness of the color will automatically lift the spirits of anyone who enters.

↑
When lighting these glowing colors, only a small amount of artificial light is needed. Use diffused light, incandescent bulbs, or firelight for beautiful atmosphere in a yellow-orange room. An overhead light might make the palette seem shockingly bright.

↖
Combine neutral elements and furnishings with the strength of yellow upholstery to keep a room lively and free-spirited. Here, a sisal rug and natural wood storage allow the bright colors to pop.

FACT FILE:

1. ORANGE IS CONSIDERED THE WARMEST HUE BECAUSE IT INCORPORATES TWO DIFFERENT HOT COLORS—YELLOW AND RED, SO THINK ABOUT COLORING A COLD, DARK SPACE WITH BRIGHT ORANGE.

2. DON'T BE AFRAID TO USE ORANGE WITH RED OR PINK; NO LONGER GARISH, THIS COMBINATION IS AN EXOTIC MIX.

3. BEWARE WHEN USING ORANGE WITH BLACK, THE EFFECT COULD BE ENERGY DRAINING WHEN APPLIED TO THE HOME.

4. BUDDHIST MONKS WEAR SAFFRON-COLORED ROBES AS A SYMBOL OF ENLIGHTENMENT, SO CONSIDER APPLYING THIS CONCEPT TO A MEDITATION ROOM.

BOLD COLOR THAT WORKS

Orange is especially useful in task-specific rooms. Consider incorporating a vibrant shade of techno-orange in the design of any room where "hardwork-ing" is the theme.

Kitchens: A warm, welcoming color that imitates the glow of a fire and radiant energy, orange stimulates the appetite.

Dark spaces: Even more specifically, orange serves as the opposite of camouflage in calling attention to itself in low light, which can be extremely helpful in tight spots.

Home offices: This color signifies work and height-ens our awareness of technology.

↗
Blue is the complement of orange. In large open spaces and one-room living, color can help differ-entiate living areas. Brightly colored open shelves also work as an eye-catching room divider. Here both ideas come together to separate a kitchen area from sleeping quarters.

→
Bold orange paired with yellow creates a central theme of warmth for living areas that are inviting and inspirational.

→
A ripe shade of orange takes the marquis in this home office that uses yellow and green as accents. Imagine that a raspberry pink and red were used instead of the colors in the desk; the overall effect would be a world apart. Here the cooler tones work hard to freshen up the sweet shade of orange.

↖
A good way to mix complementary colors is to reserve one shade for the walls and another for the furnishings and then decide how much of these shades you want to add as accents.Tip: Use your favorite on the furniture because if you hate the walls, you can always start over.

←
Orange has become one of the signature colors of new media and technology. It has been said to pro-mote awareness and an open mind, but it also has come to mean fast, easy, and fun—the catch phrase of the information age.

AMBER HUES FOR INSTANT COZINESS

Predominantly yellow-based oranges like tangerine, amber, mango, and saffron are rarely used to their fullest potential. These hues of orange can infinitely turn up the warmth in any room, without adding excessive drama or overwhelming color. Yellow-orange, red-orange, and blue-green are some of the most versatile bright colors for interiors because their mix of tones lends them a shape-shifting quality. If intense orange seems a little too bright, consider a deeper or more yellow version rather than immediately turning to the pastel variety of apricot or peach.

Yellow-oranges are the perfect choice if neither a blazing yellow nor a fiery orange seems to fit your decor. These colors work their magic on warm wood tones and enhance the patina on a worn farm table or rough-hewn ceiling beams. A sweet shade of tangerine, used in accents and furnishings, will pump up the style in a room filled with warm, earth tones like ochre and terracotta. Though still fun and modern, these colors can be easier to work with than an intense orange hue.

A saffron-colored sofa or walls washed in a warm amber add a glow that cannot be found with any of the standard brights. If you are ready to paint on the orange, but not ready for such a daring commitment, try using tangerine on larger surface areas with touches of bold orange as an accent.

→
For living areas that double as storage spaces, don't try to hide your belongings. Highlight the lot with a simple yet powerful color combination, like this dark orange with natural upholstery.

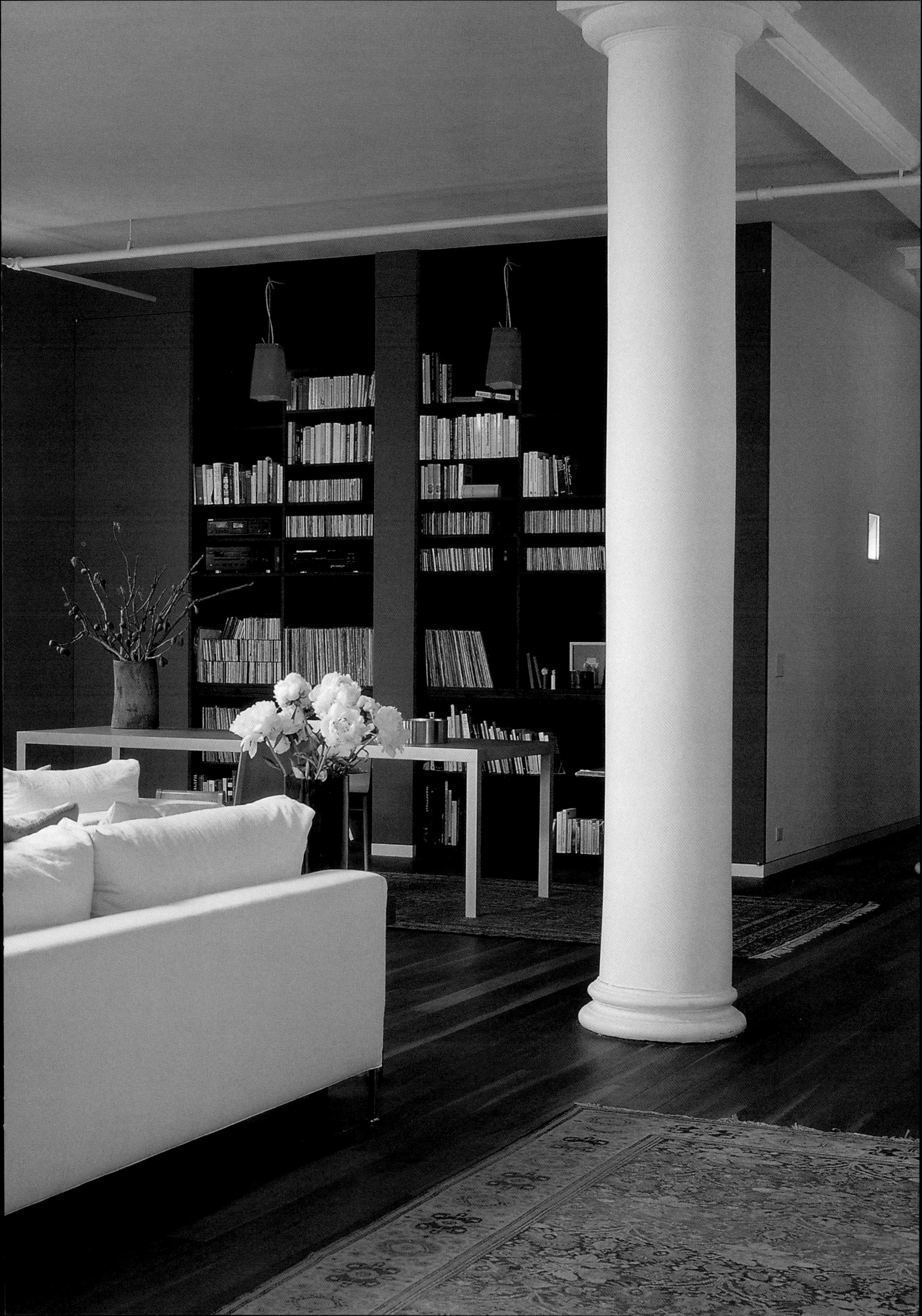

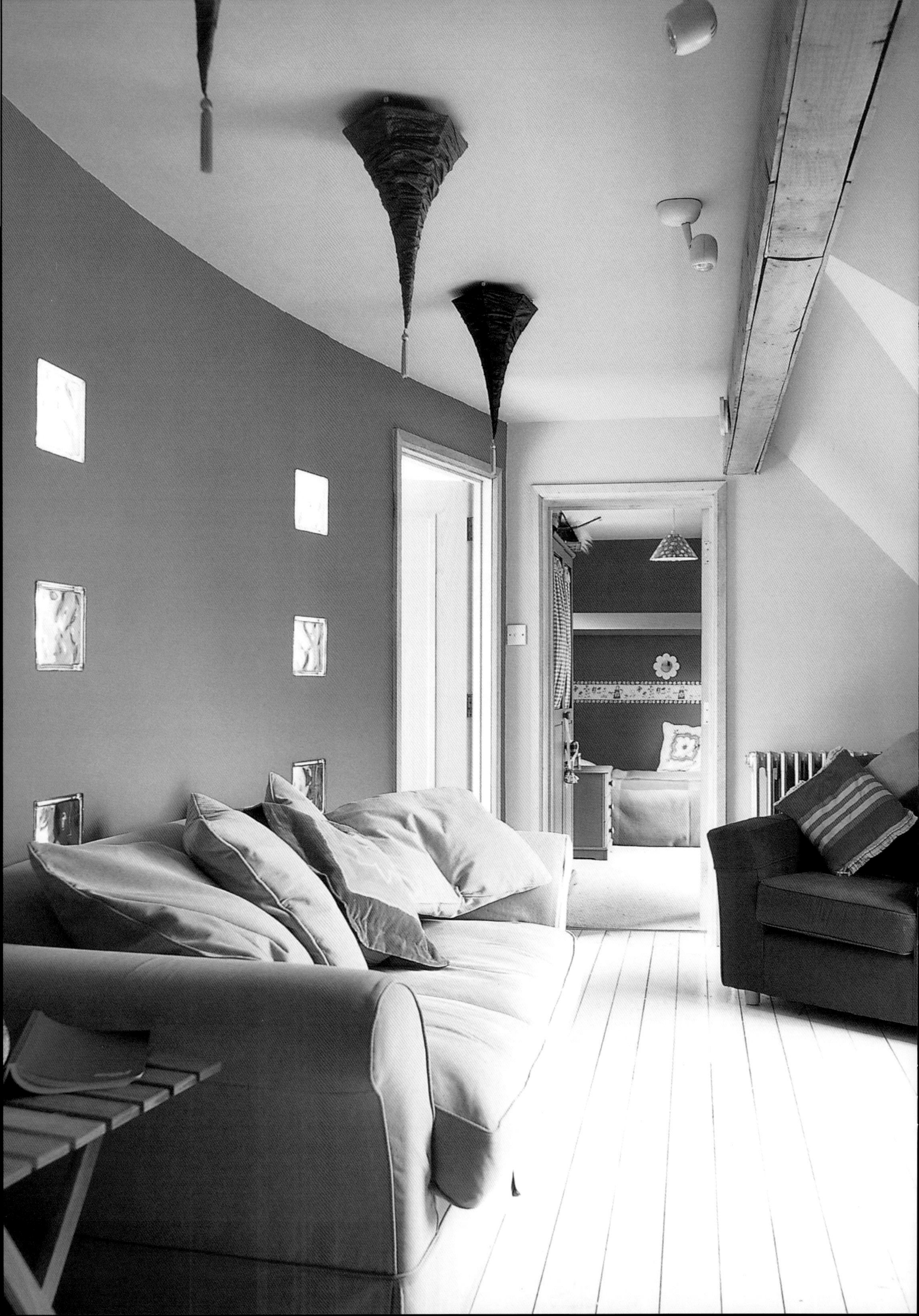

GETTING THE MIX RIGHT

If you want to use bright orange but are afraid that your decor won't be taken seriously enough, try using several different hues on either side of a true orange. Monochromatic color schemes work hard for a combined effect that feels cohesive but doesn't seem stagnant or boring: Team up persimmon with lighthearted apricot or mango. Incorporate patterns and textures for added interest. For accents, choose one or two contrasting colors so the effect doesn't get too monolithic.

Always remember that orange combines the assertive qualities of red with the sunny disposition of yellow, so a monochromatic room in orange might be too hot to handle. If your heart is set on this color, feel free to wrap a room in the brightest shade but beware that orange will excite. It makes us feel active and playful, so if you are feeling blue, an orange room will be diametrically opposed to your mood. This is why we almost never see an all-orange interior, but why it can be so much fun to experiment with. Combine a true orange with lighter shades of yellow-orange like calendula and an almost red, such as coral. Pick shades that call to mind natural combinations like a bunch of poppies or chyrsanthemum so they feel invigorating rather than artificial.

↗
It can be difficult to make a bathroom interesting but an unlikely combination of colors can quickly do the job. Orange is not the most obvious choice for a bath where we usually think of the calming, cooling shades. But here, notice how two hues add warmth, depth, and style to a simple pedestal sink.

←
Bold orange and brilliant yellow come together to show off the curves of this uniquely shaped living room. Much of this interior's success relies on the natural finish of the floor and ceiling beams that serve to ground the room. In contrast to the theatrical hanging light fixtures, natural elements and a flood of sunlight team up to keep the colors from looking too artificially flavored.

PURE ENERGY

Energetic and appetite stimulating, it is hard to avoid mentioning food with these orange hues: mango, tangerine, papaya—all have the power to infuse a professional-strength kitchen with modern warmth and welcome. In kitchens filled with cook's fantasy stainless steel and appliances, matching them with bold color is the best way to bring the space to life.

If you are looking for an extra measure of warmth, consider using a spicy palette like paprika, curry, or saffron. Match strong color with innovation by introducing brightly colored laminates or rubberized industrial flooring that is now being marketed for the home in a range of colorways and textured designs. And don't forget about new dyes and stains for wood ceilings and cabinetry; now available in orange palettes from mandarin to peach.

→

This dressmaker's studio offers a remarkable lesson in mixing bold patterns and bright colors in one space. By restricting the palette to one quarter of the color wheel, the harmonious shades don't compete with the designs.

↓

Take inspiration from fresh squeezed juice: here, the color on the walls is bold and vibrant but it doesn't demand center stage. Yellow-orange acts like a light source, brightening the area for floral arrangements, artwork, and modern fixtures.

ORANGE PLAYS WELL WITH OTHER BRIGHTS

Orange is rarely seen alone or in monochromatic schemes. This is because it harmonizes beautifully with so many other colors. With shades of blue, its complement, orange will stand boldly in contrast. With other warm hues—red, pink, yellow—orange is right at home. Make sure, though, that you combine orange with equally bright colors because the strength of this hue will steal the show when paired with weaker tints.

Let go of any fear and hesitation. If you want to use bright orange with hot pink and bold yellow, go ahead and do it rather than trying to choose shades that would be safer or more universal. These colors will work well together because they are all part of the same family of warm tones. Make sure that when using adjacent colors, you keep the number of hues around two or three—with at least one less vibrant accent color.

A warm mix of oranges, reds and pinks can create a cozy atmosphere out of a standard white box of a room. Wild color combinations drench a room. But this is not a palette for spaces that are architecturally intricate or filled with ornate designs. Patterns should be big and bold; small, busy patterns would compete with the graphic quality of the colors.

SORBET

TANGERINE

LOLLIPOP

PAPAYA

RAW SILK

PUMPKIN

MANDARIN ORANGE

ENTERTAINING ORANGE

For living rooms and spaces reserved for entertaining, orange adds a cheerful dose of fun. It's an outgoing color that can break down the barriers of formal behavior. Orange makes you feel like a kid again; use it in rooms where you'll be dining or entertaining an active group. Another benefit to using orange to entertain is that it is flattering for just about every skin tone, making people look sun-kissed and healthy.

In rooms dedicated to entertainment or new media, orange is always a bright idea. Orange is all over the Internet because it suggests fast, easy and fun—each of the Internet's best selling points. The color orange suggests newness and technology. It is claimed by colorists to help expand our minds.

For living rooms and media rooms, in particular, you will want to prevent orange from looking artificial or overly sweet. Consider adding lots of white, or employ a paler shade of yellow to keep orange fresh. Temper the sweetness of orange with pale green in order to ground this techno-bright color.

←
Wood stains are available in a rainbow of pre-mixed tints like this mandarin orange cabinetry, but you can also create your own color by adding a touch of paint to any clear varnish.

AN EXOTIC
POINT OF VIEW

For many years it has been a given that pink, red, and orange clash. This myth is shattered as home design accessories and textiles, borrowing from Eastern traditions and warm color palettes, are all catching on to these vibrant color combinations.

Like all adjacent colors, pairing hues that lie next to each other on the spectrum will usually look harmonious and feel right. For the warm colors, this means creating a cozy nook out of a room, lighting it with care, and trying to prevent the colors from getting too hot. Keep these combinations fresh with lots of white and big windows. For evening, be sure to add plenty of indirect incandescent lighting. The warm tones in these lights will provide just the right kind of glow to match the look. Fluorescent lights will destroy an all-warm palette, so don't even think about it or your colors will turn to mud. High-intensity white lights might be too powerful for a bedroom but will offer plenty of true light for workspaces.

→
Hot fuchsia window sheers let in diffused light to turn this orange living room into an exotic oasis.

→
Hot color and bold graphics team up to create an eye-catching set of curtains that barely lets on its true identity as a utility closet. Take care not to place bold, bright colors in direct sun where they might fade and be turned into a watered down version of their former selves.

DEEP ORANGE FOR INSTANT WARMTH

Dark orange is a refined way to add a dose of youthful energy. Pumpkin and coral colors are a bit more retro and, when paired with even darker and more neutral tones, these oranges stand out like a beacon of color. Add some vibrant shades of green or yellow, and deep orange will ground the room with a warm earth tone.

For the bedroom or study, a deep version of orange such as persimmon, is a nice alternative to traditionally tranquil colors. Spicy orange will automatically warm up a space by making it seem smaller and more intimate. Instead of choosing an elegant shade of dark red for your bedroom, try a more unexpected color like spicy paprika or vivid coral. Give orange a trial run in the bedroom by changing just the bedding to an invigorating shade of papaya. These colors are like red's younger sister; they won't feel as serious or sensual but are every bit as wild and equally bold.

↖
Orange as a background for yellow and white is a variation on the natural application of these colors. Bold and bright, this reversal is still harmonious but provides energetic color.

←
For neutral areas, one great expanse of color may be all you need to create a focal point and direct the eye. The headboard in this large bedroom serves as a backdrop and defines a sleeping area.

RACY REDS

Rubies, poinsettias, cinnamon, chili peppers—one only has to think of these potent objects to remind us of the power of red. It is a bold, bright, shocking color in nearly all its shades and incarnations. And, yet, somehow red is always sophisticated and passionate. It can be both cozy and intimidating, glamorous and rustic, chic and comforting. Red has a life-giving kind of forcefulness.

It's the first of the bold bright colors to be used freely in fashions for both the home and in clothing, because it has its roots in so many different cultural traditions. Red is a classic bold, a bright and vivid color that has never lost its power.

There is a certain air of extravagance about red and often times, we tend to get carried away when using it, adding more and more color until we have saturated ourselves in red. If you want to add bold color without an overbearing sense of heat, consider adding dashes of the shade in pillows, artwork or on the floor.

↑
Beautiful brocade fabrics and golden tassels are
a lovely accompaniment to red.

↖
Green is the complement to red. A mix of red with
a muted shade of green makes an understated
contrast: a paler green won't compete for attention
but still acts as a foil for any red.

FACT FILE

1. PHYSIOLOGICALLY, RED INCREASES
   HEART RATE AND METABOLISM—
   SO TRY IT OUT IN A DINING AREA OR
   A ROOM USED FOR ENTERTAINING.

2. PAIR RED WITH WHITE TO TEMPER
   THE HEAT AND PROVIDE A LIVELY
   CONTRAST THAT'S A PROVEN
   ATTENTION-GETTER.

3. IN FENG SHUI, RED IS ASSOCIATED
   WITH THE ELEMENT OF FIRE, SO
   USE IT WHEREVER YOU WANT
   MORE ENERGY AND FUEL FOR THE
   IMAGINATION SUCH AS A HOME
   OFFICE OR KITCHEN.

4. RED IS THE OLDEST COLOR; IN
   EVERY LANGUAGE, AFTER DIS-
   COVERING WORDS FOR BLACK
   AND WHITE, THE COLOR RED WAS
   GIVEN A NAME.

THE COLOR MOODS OF RED

Use red as an accent or go all the way with giant doses for entire rooms. Little items will stand out while larger applications declare a bold design statement. And, although it is a primary, red has many color moods: there are pink "watermelon" reds, screen-siren "blue" reds, near-black "lacquer" reds, and perfectly balanced "poppy" reds. Red in a room exists to impress: try Moroccan red in a dining room to stimulate taste buds, or a sensational scarlet in a living room, and velvety crimson in the boudoir—or anywhere you'd like a sensual sanctuary.

←
A natural attention-getter, red is the perfect color to use on a focal wall. Here a simple woven magazine rack feels like artwork against a flaming red wall.

← ↖
White accents will always work well with red furnishings. For a modern yet universal attraction, think of stop signs and national flags.

← ←
Temper the heat of this flaming color with a classic combination of fresh white and saturated primary red. A simple idea for taming any bright color is to pair it with white or cream particularly on the floors and trim. Here a wood floor is painted shiny white while the furnishings are kept clean and simple; mixing light wood grains with white canvas.

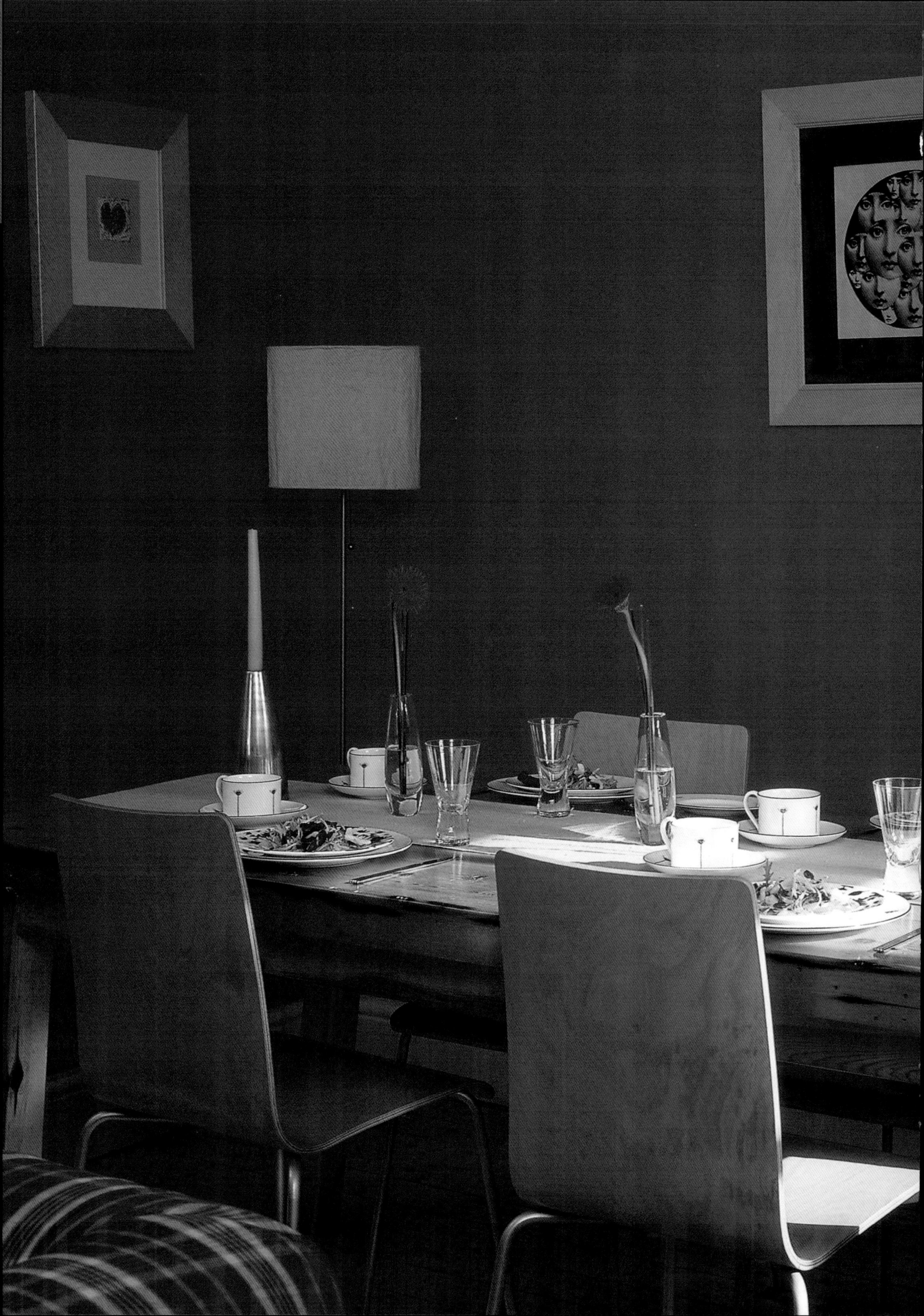

RED ALERT
DINING ROOMS

Red is a warm, uplifting, high-energy color—and the perfect choice for a dining room. Not only is it said to increase the appetite, but red also revs the metabolism. This can be a boon if you are considering using red in the dining room; it will not only make your guests hungry but it will also enhance their senses of smell and taste. As a bonus, red is an uplifting color that promotes good conversation and wildly successful dinner parties.

For the BOLDEST dining room designs, match the atmosphere you want to the hue: Consider full-bodied claret red for richness; chili pepper for heat and excitement; deep raspberry red for sleek sophistication. Whatever red you choose, keep in mind that the darker the color the more light is absorbed. A re-do in red may make you want to rethink the room's ambient lighting as well—turning up the voltage on a dark dining room.

Because bold red has such powerful suggestions of opulence and style, it's a color that designers frequently turn to for restaurant interiors. Blazing crimson provides gustatory comfort and an elegance unmatched by almost any other color. Make this design secret your own, and use it to create sleek, bistro chic in your dining room. For even more style fusion, pair red walls with lacquered black finishes on chairs and picture frames, and the look is instantly Eastern and sophisticated.

←
In an otherwise simple setting, hot chili pepper red on the walls adds a dose of heat and a sure boost to conversation. It's a daring color and, especially where furnishings are kept clean and simple, a blazing red on the walls will make every piece stand out. Be sure to match the type of red to the tones in a wood, for these light honeyed wood pieces, a red-orange works better than a red that contains any blue.

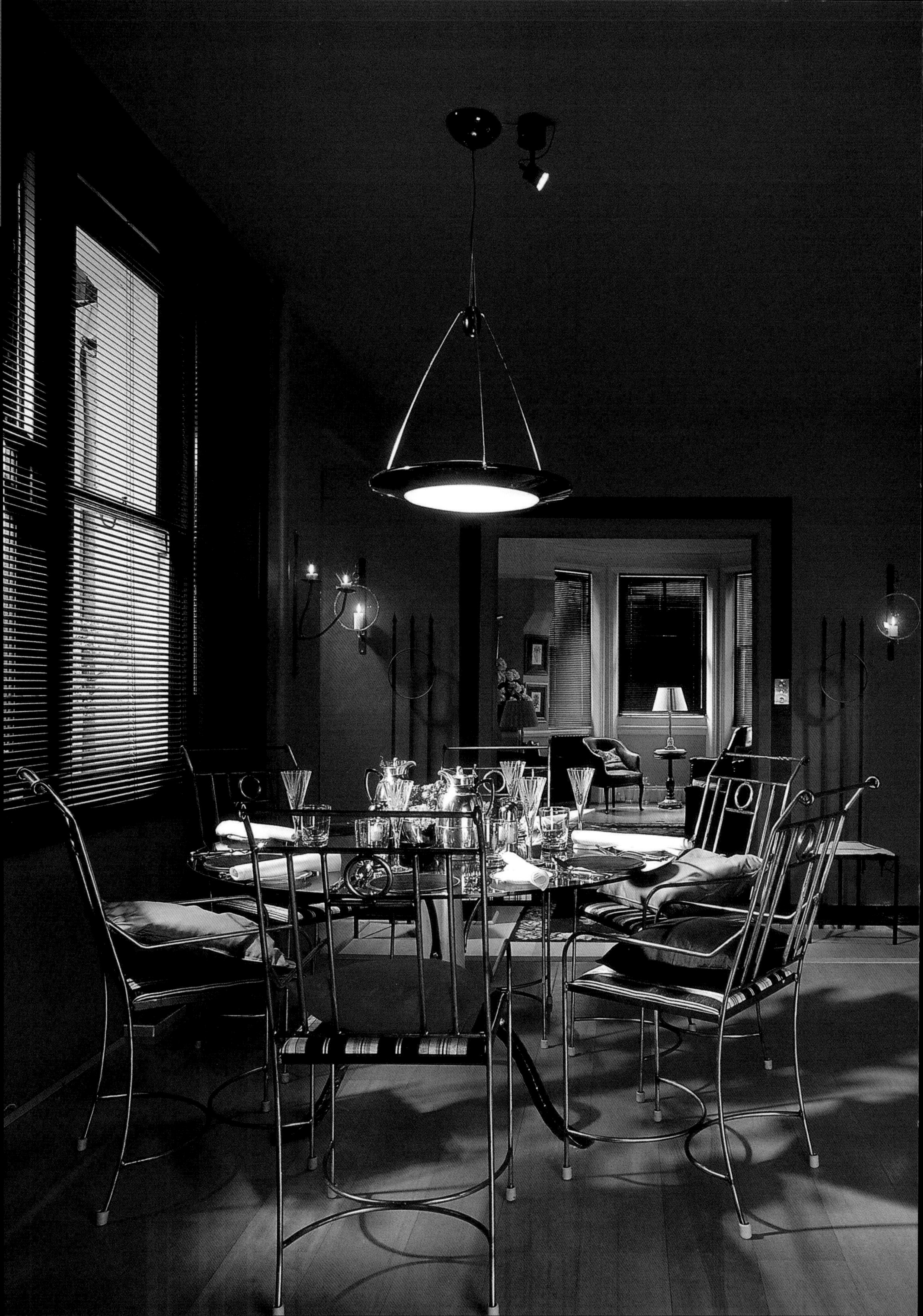

RED MAKES BEIGE BLUSH

People who love red usually REALLY love red. If this applies to you, pick a hue, whether it's the color of a matador's cape or a maraschino cherry, and use it to its fullest capacity. Some of the most frequent design mistakes are made when people get scared at the last minute and choose a shade lighter or duller than the color they are actually wanting. As a rule, choose a red paint sample that is, in fact, one shade mellower than you are looking for; after it is applied to the walls, the resulting color will seem a little bit brighter and more intense.

If you are concerned that your chosen shade might be too red hot, team it with a creamy canvas-colored white or use it in smaller doses against a neutral background. It's easy to temper the heat of a flaming red with fresh accents of white. Reds can be incorporated smoothly into a decor that consists of any of the various wood tones—Chinese red and cinnabar work well with teak and other exotic hardwoods, deeper crimsons look great with mahogany or dark-stained woods. For true reds, such as scarlet and race-car red, any raw material—whether pine, steel or concrete—are a great foil for pulsating color. Use primary reds liberally in minimal interiors for a dose of urban smart color. It's a courageous color, so it works well against daring architecture and contemporary design for a dramatic effect.

↖
Red + Black = Exotic. The rising popularity of Asian-inspired style has contributed to a new love for red and black lacquer. A successful palette for both furniture and tabletop accessories, Chinese red with black accents is a rediscovered favorite. Use this simple, graphic combination to powerful effect by working it into pared down, minimal designs.

↖
Red upholstery makes a throne out of any chair. A regency armchair, painted white, does well sheathed in a combination of red and pink fabric. Don't be afraid to use these two colors together, especially when refereed by a clean, fresh white. Red and pink make a terrific twosome.

←
In a boxy red dining room, the color on the walls matches the drama of the architectural scale. A huge room, blessed with large windows, can afford to take bold color and design details to the extreme. For a dining room that is frequently lit by candles or a fireplace, consider the daring move of painting walls and ceiling scarlet, the resulting space will reflect a fiery glow.

RED LOVES
HIGH DRAMA

Work with red in the living room for stand-out drama that can easily be balanced with versatility. Experiment with it until you perfect the mix: red lends itself to most furnishing shapes, creating instantly sexy looks with a practical, comfortable side. Supple yet sturdy, even a spot of bold red can get the message across—ease into it with a single, smashing red chair, red throw pillows, or a dashing red accent. Red is a natural attention-getter and, therefore, works well to attract attention away from what you don't like (but can't change) and toward the things you love about a room.

Try using red against black-and-white bold graphics and see the magic of the color take effect. It's a strong enough color to stand its own against wild, tricky patterns. It also seems that people who love to use red, don't like it to compete with other colors. The statement red makes is so loud and strong, that few design elements can stand up to its strength and many seem to cower in its presence.

←
Pink adds excitement to red without the intimidation. Many are afraid to use red with pink because these two colors have a reputation to clash, but design has come a long was since those rules applied.

→
Pair red with other primary colors for a look that is anything but simple. Primaries are always a sure thing together, because they are the purest forms of color. When combined, the prismatic effect of blue, yellow, and red is literally pleasing to the eye because there is no crossover in the colors to be discerned.

The red color plan is all about graphic strength: red makes objects appear to advance toward the viewer and it highlights silhouettes. Thus, red in a room will make the walls seem closer together, while it makes the atmosphere more intimate, and puts the shapes of objects into high relief. You can further enhance red's strength by using it with contrasting patterns such as a wild zebra print. The result is an eye-catching scene that will not be ignored. If you love drama, but don't like animal prints, set a single piece of a high-gloss red furniture against a black-and-white floor design for the same effect. This is a sure-fire color combination for an immediate makeover.

←
How drama plays out sometimes depends on how you set the stage. Against a backdrop of cheeky red, even meek objects bloom.

←
In a room that is awash with light, painting one key wall in a saturated hue of deep red might be enough to flood the entire space in red. Here, lots of red paint and colored glass combine to make this foyer into a pool of scarlet-colored light.

LIVE IT UP WITH RED

When considering red for a living room or common space, be sure to test drive all the options. Because red is such an intense color, consider painting a large square of your intended color on the wall. If it looks too bright or too dark, you can fix it before going all the way. Another idea is to make an "idea board" that groups together paint chips, fabric swatches, and pictures as a way of trying out various combinations. Don't forget to consider lighting as well as the size and temperature of the room.

If your room is large enough and cool enough, go ahead and turn up the heat with an all-out monochromatic look. Several different shades or textures of bright red, when combined, saturate the senses and impart a feeling of high drama. No one who enters a room that is dressed head-to-toe in fiery red will neglect to comment on the chic colors; red will not be ignored. Don't be afraid to use red with adjacent colors like pink and orange; although we've been scolded into thinking that these colors clash with red, in fact, the resulting combinations are beautifully harmonious and suggestive of Mid-Eastern ceremonies and traditional bizarres.

If all-red seems all-too-much, then work on pairing red with other colors that are equally vibrant. Match the sizzling heat of red with an awe-inspiring blue, it will not only cool down red but each color will stand out all the more in contrast. Add yellow or green to the mix, for a playful combination that feels like a comic strip.

↗
Use red as a tool to "punch out" special areas that you want to draw attention to. As the color with the highest light wave frequency, we are automatically drawn to it. The color given off by a red wall is vivid enough to bounce onto the objects surrounding it.

↗
Rooms that are flooded with light allow a greater freedom in terms of bright colors. If you are attracted to bold color, but shy of reds that shout, try using them first in a space that is brightly lit with sunlight. The entire aura of the room will feel rosy.

→
The boldest color schemes take advantage of the impression made by starkly contrasting colors: blue with orange, red and green, purple plus yellow, all compete for the most eye-catching combinations.

RED TURNS HEADS

Kitchens offer designers the freedom to have fun because they are generally such utilitarian spaces. Most kitchens need a healthy dose of color to liven up the atmosphere. Red is an ideal solution because it is such a hot, fiery color. Reminiscent of wood-burning stoves and kitchen hearths, flaming reds are a perfectly appropriate color for a kitchen. For an old-fashioned look with a bold kick, consider introducing a ruby hue instead of terracotta in a country kitchen.

With its active sense of welcome, the red palette is so right for the kitchen that it becomes hard to choose a main hue. If you'd like to stay in the more neutral zone, paprika reds work especially well with other colors. Saturated, balanced tomato red is another good option; try it in a design of small square tiles for a backsplash or in a mid-level checkerboard pattern that divides a red wall at the bottom from white on top. Smart cherry red pours on the polish—a good way to turn up the heat in a kitchen filled with standard-issue appliances. Take notes from the pros, however, and check that the amount of red will work in each season—in the warm months, a too-red kitchen is the last place anyone wants to be.

If you are replacing fixtures or appliances, the surprising news is that red is no longer off-limits. The latest addition to a rainbow of refrigerator, stove, and microwave colors available, red is pure fun in unexpected places. For an all-white kitchen, the addition of some high-speed red appliances might be the only color needed.

→

With cabinets in a hot cinnamon red, this industrial-looking kitchen warmly greets a cook and offers a dose of creativity and courage. Red is a color that really works when paired with industrial materials like stain-less steel and concrete. The reflective quality of the metal reflects the high-gloss paint on the cabinets.

CRIMSON KISS

CINNABAR

SCARLET

HOT PANTS

LIPSTICK

RITZY RED

CHINESE POPPY

VERMILION

RACECAR RED

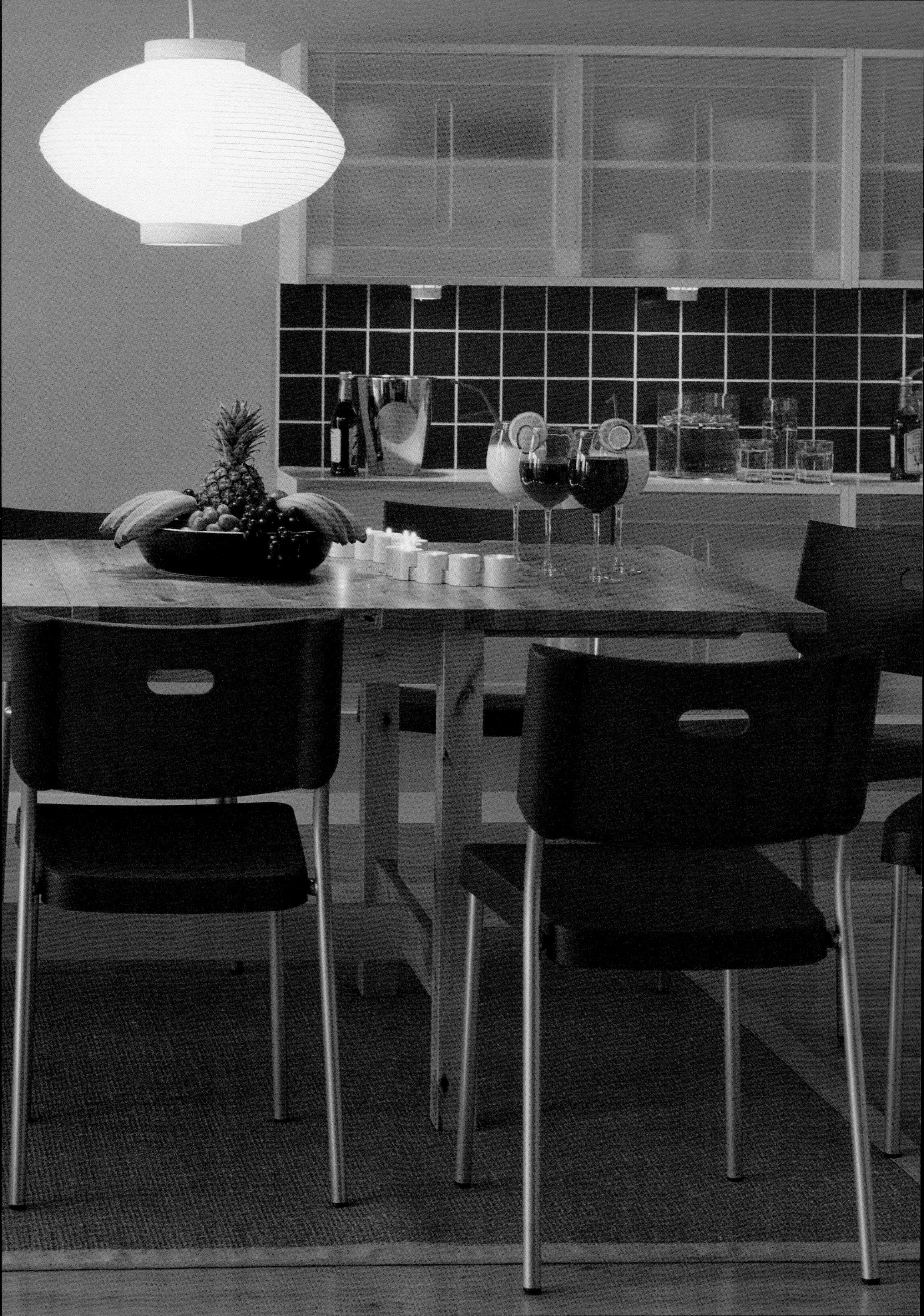

↑
Red is pure fun in unexpected places.

←
A modern kitchen in yellow and red turns the notion
of "fast-food" colors upside down. Here, this duo
looks chic and sleek.

↑
Bright colors, red especially, must be carefully lit.
Candles and well-placed spotlights are perfect for
controlling a wild color palette.

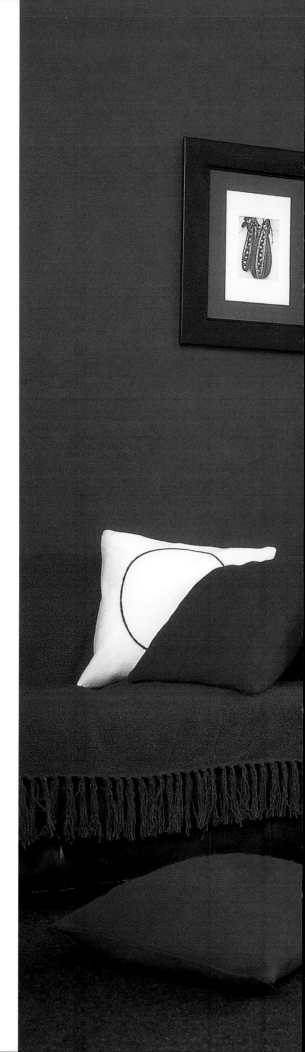

→
Monochromatic rooms in deep, vibrant reds are
great, particularly at night. A frequent recipe for
design success in nightclubs and chic restaurants,
all red rooms are always memorable. Translate this
into your own home by combining up to four different shades of red in the same number of textures
for a cozy and invigorating decor.

ATTENTION-GRABBING RED

Red is the first color that our eyes recognize; as a baby we learn to see red before seeing any other color. This is probably due to the fact that red is an advancing color; it pops out at us and calls attention to itself. When using red in the home, be sure to take advantage of this characteristic. Use it on a focal wall that draws attention to powerful architectural elements, or on a wall that holds a piece of artwork that is of particular importance. Red heralds greatness. It is the signature color of power and sophistication, and many successful people have learned to harness the power of red and use this classic, bold color to their advantage.

When lighting red, be sure to use incandescent lights or any bulb with a warm base color. Fluorescent lights may take the warmth out of the color leaving it looking like a muddy brown or nearly green. A halogen lamp would work well for a dreary afternoon, but for evening a brightly lit red may be a bit overpowering. Consider using several different light sources for different times of day for a vivid red. Low-wattage incandescent, or even pink bulbs, would work best for evening (in lieu of firelight,) while exposed windows or a skylight are perfect for sunny climates. If your climate is cold and dreary, red will work hard to warm it up but you may want to have some bright, white light to simulate the sun.

INTIMATE RED

An invigorating shade of bright red can set anyone's pulse racing but it can also be a place for comfort and warmth. Because red creates an intimate atmosphere, a bedroom enveloped in this sultry hue is at once daring and inviting. Red often makes for a contradiction when used subtly because it is a color that is far from subtle. Combine it with traditional bedroom elements or cool it down with large doses of fresh white for a bedroom that is sexy but never brazen.

The greatest thing about red in sleeping spaces is its gender-neutral stance. The perfect hue for shared rooms, red makes both men and women feel the power of love. Red is essentially the color of romance though we tend to associate pink with those characteristics: Remember that red is the purest and most saturated form of pink. If you love hot pinks but your partner doesn't, try turning to red and matching it with pale petal pinks to soften the effect so you both get your way. This combination of red with pink is ideal for a bedroom because it combines the power of red with the nurturing qualities of pink for a feeling of secure coziness.

→
Red is a perfect bedroom color for people who look good wearing red. Whenever choosing colors for the bedroom whether its for the walls or your sheets, always be prepared to "try on" the color yourself. It is essential that we surround ourselves in a bedroom with colors that match our complexions.

RED LOOKS HOT

When you start using red, it can tend toward extravagance and high drama. If this is the feeling you are looking for, you are in luck but, if not, be careful to use whatever restraint you can muster. In the bedrooms on the previous pages, the color red has been used to its most scintillating capacity. Color forecasters often predict the periods when red is in high fashion by the aura of confidence in the air. This is the feeling that is most often associated with red, so it seems only logical that when people begin to use red, their confidence soars, and they end up going farther than they ever imagined; painting ceilings and incorporating wild textures and patterns.

SHOCKING PINK AND PURPLE

DARE TO BE VIBRANT

The span of colors between hot pink and bold purple are the most daring of all the vibrant hues because they are rarely applied in interiors. Home furnishings designers have been using lots of bold primary colors in the last two decades and oranges most recently, but pink and purples seem to be farthest down on the mainstream curve. Consider yourself at the frontier of design when deciding on a palette of vibrant pink or purple. There is no point in being timid with these fabulous hues, in wild, encompassing design statements or as a single bold streak applied liberally to a living room sofa or short expanse of hallway.

There are really no rules with the pink/purple palette, because these hues make up an elusive range. In fact, designers sometimes call them the "imaginary" colors, as they fall outside the traditional spectrum. They form the connection between red and indigo and so they are "outside" the rainbow. Of course, this is what makes hot pink and purple such appealing colors to use; they remind us of a fantasy world, a place where creativity is not problem-solving but pretend.

↑
Combine purples with adjacent pinks for an almost monochromatic color scheme. These colors remind us of softly scented flowers and springtime but these are not little-girl pastels. When used in metallic form or some other daring texture, traditionally disdained Easter-egg colors become bright, bold and never boring.

↖
Give hot-house-rose a natural boost by adding accents of green. Choose colors that might be found together in nature to ground a vibrant shade of pink — or simply add outdoorsy elements, such as the sisal rug and framed leaves pictured here, to calm pink without making it drab.

FACT FILE:

1. HOT PINKS, LIKE RED, ARE ADVANC-
   ING COLORS THAT MAKE OBJECTS
   SEEM CLOSER. BUT HOT PINK HAS
   AN ADDED SENSE OF GOOD HUMOR
   THAT IS ALL ITS OWN.

2. UNIQUE PURPLE COMBINES THE
   PERSONALITIES OF TWO OPPOSING
   PRIMARY COLORS: RED AND BLUE.
   IT WORKS BEST IN AREAS DEDI-
   CATED TO CREATIVITY, SUCH AS
   A STUDY OR STUDIO.

3. TRUE PINKS ARE GREAT FOR A BED-
   ROOM BECAUSE THEY REPRESENT
   LOVE, ROMANCE, AND HIGH STYLE.

4. PAIR SORBET-COLORED PINKS AND
   PURPLES TOGETHER FOR A FANTASY-
   FILLED DESIGN STATEMENT.

5. THE LIGHTER SIDE OF THIS PALETTE
   IS SOFT WITHOUT BEING SHY: USE
   TINTS OF PINK AND PURPLE FOR A
   FLORAL SENSE WITH A MOD TWIST.

This color range is the perfect choice for a bold makeover—even if you change little else about a room, adding pink and purple will make an instant style statement. Consider hot pink to turn a standard bedroom into a sassy and sultry destination; vivid lavender to make a bath soothing and inviting; rose-colored walls for updated living spaces filled with comfort. Steal from confectionary colors to suggest kitschy fun, or add a coat of bold purple paint to inspire a home office. This is the palette of confident people: Use it to show your level of comfort, or to find new daring in your everyday endeavors.

↑
To keep colors from clashing, add a few well-placed neutral elements. The gray on the wall makes a perfect backdrop to the two-toned loveseat here. If gray is not on your color scope—a creamy white will work just as well.

←
Aromatherapy candles work beautifully in rooms that use harmonizing colors—sweet smelling lavender and freesia candles double the effect of a pale purple bath.

↑
Softer shades of pink don't have to look dull. Mix
and match several shades and textures for a sophisticated living area.

RED WITH PINK: CLASH OF THE DIVAS

Next to red, hot pinks sizzle. Not the bubblegum pinks and cotton candy colors of a frilly bedroom, but a more daring palette of fuchsia, magenta, and shocking pink. In living spaces, when we think of pink, we resort to a pastel hue of red tinted with white: magenta, on the other hand, gets its power from red but blends it with a touch of blue and barely any white. The result is cooler than true red but able to turn up the heat instantly in any situation.

Hot pinks create an entirely different atmosphere than other pinks. The hottest of them all, magenta, is passionate and intense. Magenta never fails to draw attention, so use it as a powerful accent in a contemporary design scheme or with pieces of modern art. In a bold room design, magenta comes forward as unique and full of surprises.

When using this spirited shade, go all out. Combine hot pink with red for a battle of the divas. Experiment with intensity to find harmony between the two hues, otherwise they will clash loudly. Don't get discouraged, pairing pink and red can be tricky, but it is worth it—this duet can also be one of the most powerful combinations for the home. If you are having trouble striking a balance, add touches of non-colors like white, gray, or the palest hint of creamy pink to freshen up the space and keep the palette from getting overheated.

A living room enveloped in floor-to-ceiling brights may become a difficult place to relax, not to mention a place that will make timid visitors blush. A better recipe would be to mix brights into the design in equal parts, and not let them take up more than half of the room's decor. Furnish the other half in neutral, non-colors and tie it all together with small accents of an adjacent color such as purple or orange. The satisfying result will let the strong colors create a wild play against a more soothing background.

↑
Pink works exceptionally well in monochromatic palettes because it is a tint, rather than a color. It is based on one color—red—and, therefore, will go harmoniously with any other color that contains red, its base color.

→
In order to prevent a look that isn't too flat when using a lot of pretty pink, try adding grown-up textures and details like this velvet chenille coverlet or a drop-crystal sconce. The effect will be sensual bet still innocent and charming.

PINK AND LIGHT

Pink works well in interiors because it reflects a healthy glow for every skin tone. Designers frequently suggest replacing regular white lights with soft pink light bulbs to set a flattering stage for any room. If you want to use lots of pink, it is less jarring to use soft pink lighting or lampshades lined with pink. A harsh white light may make saturated, bright pinks look too loud for a sleeping space. Stained glass lampshades and colored crystal sconces are a great way to add a rosy hue that goes beautifully with the warm tones of a pink bedroom.

→

Take pink to heights of exoticism by spicing up the rest of the room with elements that add depth and interest. Try using Chinese paper lanterns or an Indian sari draped over an armchair for a worldly touch.

THROW OUT ALL THE RULES BUT ONE

Throw all the rules about certain colors for certain spaces away—but keep the designers "four-shades" rule when using the pink palette—lest the overall effect gets too lusty. Designers suggest picking no more than four shades of a single color when developing a monochromatic palette. Choose four colors that run the gamut from a soft ballet slipper to a pulsating hot fuchsia for a confectionary of color. Adding more shades or lots of various ornamental details in a monochromatic living room will make color harmony near-impossible. These types of palettes work best in rooms with clean, modern lines so that the powerful colors can be the point of attention. But the balance is tricky; make sure that the shapes and textures are bold enough to compete with a shocking color like hot pink.

←
When applied liberally in the boldest of shades of shocking pink, the effect is anything but traditional. Mis-matched framed paintings, slipcovers, and a collection of objects sit well when seen against a backdrop of hot fuchsia.

VIVID PINK TRANSFORMS

Pink has always leaned toward the feminine in traditional design. It also carries some associations with sweet-smelling flowers and romantic decorations. Vivid pink is fun to decorate with because it retains a sense of innocence and romance, but brings along a more modern viewpoint that is substantial, strong, and bold. Consider bright pink to infuse a room with energy without the worry that the atmosphere will suddenly become too intense or too hot. Unlike deep red, a vivid pink can be sexy and passionate without being brazen.

Prettiness may be the keyword for most pinks, but pInks In the bold range have star power. Use wild pink with abandon to make a rosy Hollywood-starlet boudoir suited to your modern lifestyle. The all-pink bedroom can't help but take inspiration from these movie star bedrooms and their sensual mystique with pink silk slippers atop a fluffy fur rug and an enormous bed covered in quilted satin. In all of its incarnations, pink begs to be touched. Take advantage of this quality by combining the hue with layers of interesting textures. Don't let the walls be the only application—consider using silky textiles and lacquer furniture bathed in pink.

→
In rooms decorated with vivid pink, unconventional design seems appropo. A bed placed in the center of a room, an extra-tall nightstand, and globe light fixture all look at home in this pink bedroom.

IN THE PINK

Try covering your windows with a hot pink sheer rather than standard cream and the whole room will glow in a flood of unexpected rosiness. In small doses, pink is like the boa-clad star of the show. In larger applications, hot pink becomes the fabulous, over-the-top diva. Turn both of these qualities to great advantage in hum-drum spaces such as the laundry area or storage room: transform them with a witty pink take on a striped cabana.

If even the quick repaint is beyond your schedule, forage for bright pink throw pillows, table lamps, and accessories. Pink stands out, so it is worth it to add a quick splash of color (to any room that needs it) by replacing something standard with its flamingo-colored version. Even electronics dressed in pink are unexpectedly charming: stereos, cell phones, and cameras all look surprisingly pretty in pink.

↓
A single beautiful piece of fabric in a bold color is all it takes to create a fun and unique decor. This gently striped fabric in various pinks and orange is used as an alternative to the standard pastel sheers used for roman blinds.

FASHIONABLE PINK FOR FASHIONABLE LADIES

"To women everywhere: Banish the Black, Burn the Blue, and Bury the Beige... From now on, girls, THINK PINK!!!" declares Maggie Prescott, editor of the fictional *Quality* Magazine, in the classic Audrey Hepburn film, *Funny Face*.

Pink, in any of its variations, makes a powerful style statement. Pink has pushed out of the confines of sweet and innocent and has become a bold, sexy signature color that is not just for good girls anymore. As pink becomes a standard in high fashion, home design is only a few paces behind. Before pink becomes prêt a porter for the living room, why not use this couture color for its fullest shock value?

A hot pink rug and fuchsia furniture against white walls and light-colored flooring makes for an undeniably sassy living room. Pink has attitude wherever it is used so break all the rules about "appetizing colors." Use bubblegum pink in a kitchen or dining room for a sweet shot of irreverence. Pink tends to be a little more traditional for a bathroom or bedroom but when applied liberally in the boldest shades of shocking pink, the effect is anything but traditional. Pink will make its way into our everyday life as soon as we all get tired of the vogue for silvery shades and stone-colored neutrals. Until then, use pink in places that could use a little extra kick.

↖
If you are stuck with an all-white bathroom and want to add a dose of cheer, work in some bright elements of color that will stand out against an expanse of empty canvas. It is usually a good idea to match similar textures like the shiny laminate and chrome on this multi-tiered cart with its slick white background.

←
The laundry area seen here defies our standards by turning housework into a witty take on a striped cabana. Vibrant pink performs for us by setting the stage more dramatically than any other color.

SHOCKING PINK IN PUBLIC PLACES

↑
Hot fuchsia window sheers let in diffused light to turn this orange living room into an exotic oasis.

Don't make the mistake of confining pink to the bedroom and the bath. Every time pink makes a comeback in the fashion world, we are reminded that "it's the navy blue of India." Celebrate it in the living room and bring vibrant pinks into common spaces. Reinvent the country-house look with vivid pink. This color adds excitement to a room without feeling intimidating. Visitors will become more lively and talkative when they enter a living room filled with bright pink furnishings or boldly textured fuchsia fabrics. Hot pink carries such an inherently bold message that the courage tends to wear off on people surrounded by it.

If you want a couture effect without going all the way, try adding subtle splashes of color with floor pillows in magenta shantung silk or a mohair throw. For spaces such as hallways or entrances, bold colors make a daring statement without having to compete with furniture for attention. When you have the freedom of an essentially empty space, try painting the walls with a variegated wash or faux finish in an unexpected shade of hot pink. The result will be an exciting flash of fun color in an otherwise boring hallway or foyer.

If you love wild patterns as much as you love the color pink (as is often the case), finding the delicate balance between chic and cheap can be hard. Stave off any problems by mixing hot pink with only one or two other colors and tying them together with a brilliant pattern that incorporates all shades. For a funky, almost dollhouse effect, bring in a vibrant salmon pink and freshen it by adding an equally intense shade of its complement, lime green. Use patterned fabric in upholstered pieces or curtains to pull the colors together. Orange or turquoise also work well with hot pink. The best advice when using contrasting colors with pink is "Stay bold!" If you get nervous and try to tone down the colors, the overall look will pale and fail.

BUBBLEGUM

BLUSHING

FUCHSIA

RASPBERRY

SIZZLING PINK

AUBERGINE

LILAC

GRAPE POPSICLE

LIZ'S LOOK

PURPLE FEELS MYSTERIOUS

Purple is a very unique color. As a combination of blue and red pigments, purple has dual personalities depending on the ratio of these two colors. Cooler purples like grape and violet contain more blue than red, while warmer shades, such as orchid and aubergine, contain more red than blue. This constant duplicity, a push and pull between the two strongest, opposing colors, makes purple very difficult to control. A bold purple has the combined strength of energizing red and mellowing blue so the result is ambivalent though never neutral and always magical.

Purple, like any of the secondary colors, has a wide selection of shades. It can range from the darkest plum to the palest lavender with the effect of each shade changing dramatically. Some purples are used more conventionally in the home; aubergine makes frequent appearances in dining rooms and pale lilacs often show up in formal living rooms. The colors that create the most eye-popping, overall look are the vivid shades not frequently used in interiors.

If you like them, don't hesitate to use true purples. A grape color on living room walls can punch out pale, modern furnishings or white plaster details because it is such an unexpected and dramatic color. Like pink, purple has not yet made the mainstream home fashion circuit in its truest forms (except for a brief stint in the eighties where it fully enveloped my sister Kate's bedroom). If you are nervous to make the leap, try using purple upholstery as an accent in a hot pink or pale orchid room, the similarities between the colors will make the bold purple seem less foreign.

The other way to adapt purple for home use is to pair it with white or cream. A red/purple such as plum or bright orchid will work best with a warm cream and the more blue shades like violet and indigo will be complemented by an icier white. Either way, the freshness of white against purple brings the color back to earth while still harnessing its ethereal powers. Use this combination in rooms where imagination reigns supreme, such as a study or a room used for entertaining, and discover the magical effects of purple.

↑
Purple can be a tricky color to work with because it varies so much under different lighting. Indoor lighting can easily turn true purples into a muddied brown. Purple will appear the most true under medium intensity white lights, like halogen bulbs.

→
Designers frequently use purple in places they want to reserve for special situations. Purple feels exotic because we rarely use it in its truest form. Accentuate this quality by combining shapes and forms, as shown here.

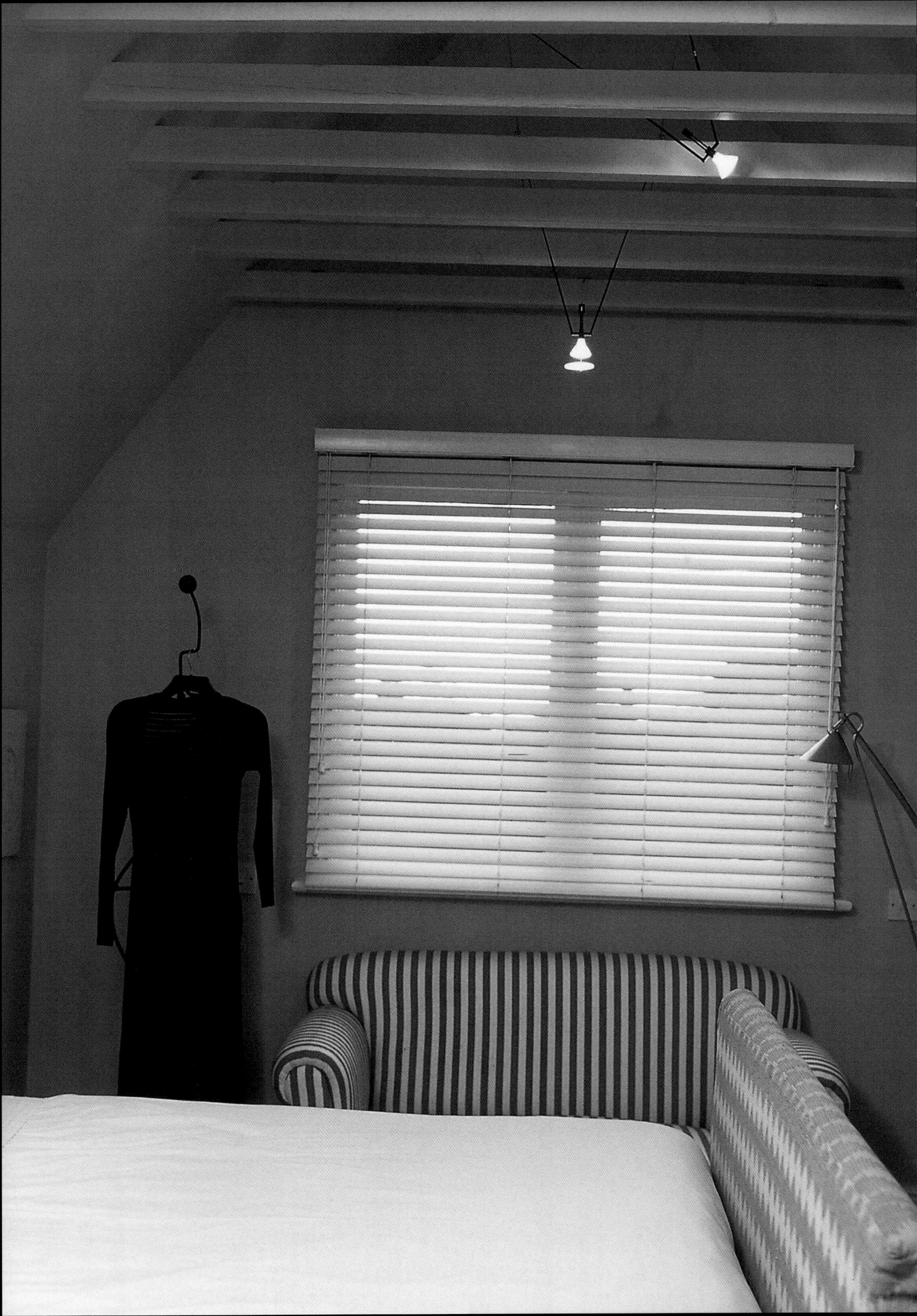

LAVENDER FOR SPECIAL PLACES

Purple is a color associated with creativity, imagination, and, in its deepest shades, royalty. In its lighter forms, purple is connected with meditation and calming environments. It makes the perfect color for a relaxing bedroom because purple combines the restful qualities of blue with the soothing element of warm pinks. But don't think lighter means dull or boring, in the case of purple, a medium lavender is anything but an insipid pastel because it combines the saturation of two opposing hues.

As a test, try replacing your bed linens (the ones that don't show) with a vivid shade of lavender. If it makes getting into bed feel appropriately soothing, consider using this color for your entire bedroom. The rule that walls should be one shade lighter than the color you have chosen, does not apply for people who thrive on bold colors. Envelope the entire room in this color, ceiling and floors included, for a sleeping space that feels like the moment when dusk descends.

If an envelope of dusk seems a bit too dramatic, consider using wild accents and fabrics to break up the color in a purple bedroom. Purple is one of the only colors that can get away with iridescent and metallic finishes in the home because it is such an imaginative color, already. Sheer purple fabrics with flecks of glitter or silver thread make a fantasy window. The same treatment can easily be created on the walls with some of the new sparkle paint finishes and iridescent glazes. Faux finishes, animal prints, and stenciling will work just as hard to compete with a brilliant shade of purple. When using this creative color, let it inspire you to decorate with an artistic hand.

←
This medium shade of purple is hard to define as either warm or cool, it seems to be somewhere in between the two temperatures and so it is also neither an advancing or receding color. Balanced directly between these two forces, purples is the only color that does not affect our body temperature.

SOOTHING PURPLE FOR BATHROOMS

↑
Softly scented lavender oil is often used for a relaxing bath; here that notion is translated into a two-toned lavender bathroom with white fixtures.

The coolest shades of purple are the most meditative. From a deep indigo to a paler periwinkle, these colors work much like calming blues but with an extra hint of warmth. This makes them the perfect color for a bathroom where the water colors work because of their appropriate associations. But these cool colors such as blue and aqua can get a little chilly in colder climates or darkly lit bathrooms covered in tiles.

These colors add that extra bit of warmth to a cold bathroom and carry associations of softly scented flowers when used in shades of hyacinth, violet, and lavender. Orchid, a pinkish purple, also works beautifully in a bathroom. Pair these flower colors with a leafy green for a clean, fresh look. Green seems to be purple's natural companion, so at the very least, open the shades to reveal outdoor greenery in a purple room. Or consider a green-tinted glass for a glass-enclosed shower. In fact, anywhere there is glass, the green/purple combination is a bright idea. In the dining room, amethyst glassware and sage green pottery has a classic but bold appeal.

Purple would also look great in a bathroom as accents against an already cool, blue or turquoise palette. All three adjacent colors, purple, blue, and turquoise could harmonize together for an intrinsically soothing bathroom. Or try pairing purple tiles with white and chrome-finished fixtures to create a cool, glittering effect. The possibilities for purple bathrooms are endless because of its clear, mystical, and softly scented qualities.

→
From a deep indigo to a paler periwinkle, purples work much like calming blues but with an extra hint of warmth. This makes them the perfect color for a bathroom where the blue water associations combine with a hot rosy glow.

COOL BLUES

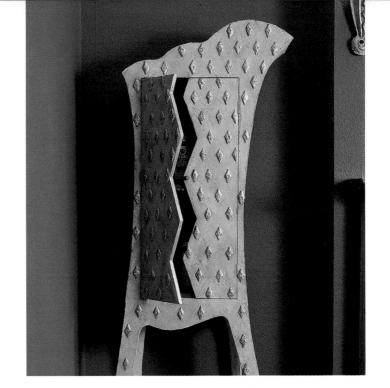

Tried and true, blue is a color that works just as well in a contemporary kitchen with sleek, shiny appliances as it does in the traditional dining room with classic blue and white china patterns. Don't underestimate the effects of blue just because it's the number one favorite color and has been for the last century. Blue has the added bonus of being a psychically connected color. It calls to mind images of the sea and the sky—and the deep blue distance in both of those elements. Blue is the color of the unknown and so it's mystical properties are passed along with every application.

Consider using cool, confident blues in places where you want to feel calm. They are proven to reduce anxiety so go ahead and use a bright electric blue and have no fear that it will be too overwhelming for your tepid guests. As a peaceful color that reminds us of cool waters, blue is an ideal color for a bathroom where it cools down a hot bath. As a fresh, trustworthy and calming color, it also works for a relaxing bedroom. But just because blue has soothing effects on our minds, don't think you have to use it in the quiet hues that seem to match those moods. Even a deep marine blue or a blazing cobalt will tend to open up and cool down a space so that it imparts a sense of freedom. Blue—particularly metallic blues—are turning out to be the color of the new millennium.

↑
Punch out brilliant shapes and textures with bold colors. A bright blue can set off almost any other bold color, with the exception of a royal purple or a hot pink. Every other shade, when combined with an equally bold blue, will stand out as the background recedes but adds interest.

↖
Blue is a receding color, so this smallish kitchen seems like a spacious work area for a fun-loving cook. The perspective from the graphic tiles on the floor, adds to the illusion of largeness perceived from the deep blue walls. Meanwhile, the red and yellow accents pop forward on first glance and we register them immediately.

FACT FILE:

1. BLUE IS A UNIVERSAL FAVORITE AND CALMING COLOR SO USE IT WHEREVER THERE ARE NEGOTIATIONS OR COMPROMISES TO MEET.

2. BLUE WORKS BEST IN THE BATHROOM BECAUSE IT CALLS TO MIND VISIONS OF THE SEA.

3. ULTRAMARINE AND COBALT PIGMENTS ARE SOME OF THE MOST PRICELESS COLORS BECAUSE THEY PROVIDE SUCH SATURATED COVERAGE WHEN TRANSFERRED INTO PAINTS...THEY ARE THE LONGEST LASTING, TOO!

4. ELECTRIC BLUE IS THE PERFECT MATCH FOR NEW MATERIALS AND INDUSTRIAL DECORS, BECAUSE IT FEELS LIKE A HIGH-TECH COLOR.

A blazing blue is perfect for living rooms, public spaces, and places for entertaining because most visitors will like the color. Whether you are planning to use a haughty peacock blue or a blaring electric blue or even one of the truer hues, blues have the largest universal appeal. Pump up your spouse's traditional sofa or brown recliner with a hefty dose of cobalt blue and chances are, you won't hear any complaints. (And when they're used to it, add a splash of red, orange, or bright green to spice it up a little.)

Not only is blue a universally popular color, but it also has the benefits of good psychic effects. In voodoo cultures, blue is thought to ward away evil spirits. For this reason, houses in neighborhoods from New Orleans to Tahiti have washed-out blue doorways and window frames. All over the old neighborhoods of New England, you can still see wraparound porches with a unique shade of pale blue-green on the ceilings. There, blue keeps the wasps and bees away. Whether these myths are true or not, blue makes a colorful statement for an exterior.

←
When we think of combining primary colors, we often are turned off by the "pre-school" factor. Blue, red and yellow as a trio often refer to children's playrooms and toys, but when used in shades just one step darker than our traditional primaries, the effect becomes sophisticated and elegant. In this living room, understated doses of bold color add interest to the room without overtaking the luxury.

← ↖
Instead of investing in an expensive china cabinet or glassed-in breakfront, try housing china in a movable closet. For a more traditional look, cover the front panels in a classic fabric and spray paint the entire thing in a eye-popping periwinkle. Against a cobalt background, this little hutch is cute and stylish.

← ←
This kitchen, enveloped entirely in a saturated cobalt, uses color to the best of its ability. With white cabinetry and accents, the brilliant colors play off each other and feel fresh and tropical. When teaming bold colors together, a winning combination uses two or three colors of equal intensity set off with gleaming white design elements.

OCEANS OF BLUE FOR THE BATHROOM

Blue is the color of the ocean and the color we associate with water, making it the perfect choice for a bathroom. Keep in mind your dreams of the perfect bathing experience: Is it a lap pool at dawn or a tropical cove on a desert island? Use your fantasies as inspiration for a bathroom or bedroom palette—from a deep blue lake at twilight to the cool turquoise waters of the Mediterranean. These private spaces are solely for your own satisfaction so don't worry about offending others' sensibilities; it's your sanctuary so make it as bold and blue as you would like.

Try using a combination of several different water-inspired blues for a cool bathroom in a hot climate or well-lit location. The perfect environment for a steamy soak in the tub is a bathroom enveloped entirely in tiles that range in color from a deep sapphire to vibrant marine blues to icier shades of light blue and white. For an even bolder look, try using two of the more contrasting shades of water colors; combine the deepest blue with a sporty shade of bright turquoise and freshen it up with touches of tactile white tile. These cool shades are the ideal remedy for tired bodies and overworked eyes, providing a space-giving and cooling environment.

↖
Tiles in the colors of the ocean and the sky are the coolest way to impart a sense of refreshment and clarity to a bathroom. As an alternative to the hospital all-white tiled bath, a palette of marina blues are soothing as well as clean looking. Use one-inch mosaic tiles, like these, to create a pattern reminiscent of breaking ocean waves or a shimmering wall of rain.

↖
Incorporating several shades of blue is one of the best ways to use this color in the bathroom because it feels like a natural application of water colors; shifting and shimmering in different kinds of light, pools of water are made up of many different reflections of blues and greens.

←
For a look that uses the color of your bathing fantasies, include the entire palette of your dream seaside: Here the memories of a Nantucket beach is brought home with painted wainscoting and a vintage tub in French blue surrounded by a collection of seawater-smoothed rocks and a weathered chair. Try using sea shell pinks and peaches or the colors of bright purples and iridescent colors of deep-sea life.

IN-HOUSE SPAS

The latest craze in spa therapies and well-being centers has brought great attention to the design of residential bathrooms. Once considered unimportant, bathrooms have become an integral part of the home and an increasingly private enclave, particularly the master bath. When opening up the bathroom to the bedroom, the use of an appropriate color scheme is essential. Powerful blues and bluegreens will help make a transition from soothing sleeping area to cool bathing sanctuary. Of course, just because you want your bath to be a place for relaxation doesn't mean that you are restricted to peaceful pastels. The more brilliant the blue, the more aquatic and marine-like it becomes, especially when paired with fresh whites.

←

Opening up the bathroom to other areas in the home is a daring idea but can be dealt with easily through the use of dividing walls, glass blocks and sliding doors. Use a water-colored palette to ease the transition from one soothing space to another. Also consider, adding a sitting area to a large bathroom, so that it may be enjoyed by one or more people in an environment of comfort and luxury.

LIGHTING BLUE BATHROOMS FOR A WARM FEELING

Blue is a cooling shade and a color that recedes, making spaces seem larger and a bit colder. In a bathroom, more than any other room, where we are regularly getting out of a steamy bath, the temperature of the colors becomes a critical consideration. So, be sure that your all-blue bathroom is warmly lit or you'll need to crank up the heat. It's best to use blue to its fullest capacity in a space that seems too small or cramped and tends to get overly steamy during long showers. Use blue in spaces that are meant to feel cool and spacious, like a poolside shower or bathroom in a tropical climate. If it still feels a bit too cold, temper the blue with touches of warm lavender and bright yellows.

Warmth in a blue bathroom can be achieved with lots of sun exposure or well-placed lighting and in many cases, both. A skylight will flood a bathroom with light during the day. The same is true for the giant picture windows that are becoming more and more popular as vantage points from soaking tubs. It is a fairly recent design idea to bring the outdoors in with showers that open up to a private outdoor room or large bay windows over a sink rather than a mirrored medicine cabinet. As long as you feel privately secure, the idea of merging the bathroom with nature, is a natural progression of the recent bathroom trends.

Open expanses of windows, however, can leave a cool blue bathroom feeling cold and dark in the evening; so be sure to compensate for daytime sun exposure with an adequate nighttime lighting system. It is also a good idea to have shades to draw as night approaches to make the room seem cozier and more protected. Aside from specially designed heat lamps, there is a multitude of lighting techniques to make blue tiles feel warmer to the touch in winter and a bright blue wall more vibrant in the morning. Adding a series of halogen spotlights will actually warm the surfaces beneath them and make porcelain or stainless feel much more touchable.

←

As we begin to see more translucent materials in the bathroom and bolder colors, we realize that our concepts for this room have become much more inspired in recent years. Glass-enclosed showers and brightly colored acrylics have taken the place of reflective wallpaper and mirrored surfaces. Electric blue with glass and chrome is a great recipe for an innovative bathroom design.

→

New materials for the bathroom include these highly durable surfacing materials that come in a rainbow of high-gloss bold colors as well as metallics. Other bathroom innovators have used photosensitive glass for shower stalls that remains transparent but turns foggy at the turn of a switch. Bright blue is the perfect color for a bathroom that uses these new products because it imparts a sense of newness and technology.

↑
This shade of periwinkle blue incorporates a touch of warmth so it doesn't seem as cold as a true primary blue; this also allows it to work with the warmer metal tones of the brass-framed mirror and bed. True blues tend to work better with silver and platinum metallics, while warmer colors work best with gold, copper and brass.

BEDROOMS
FOR PEACEFUL
SLEEPING

In the same way that this color works for a soothing bathroom, a vibrant blue is a highly appropriate shade for a restful bedroom. Think of blue and white mattress ticking and classic Laura Ashley prints in cornflower blue; now translate those traditional schemes to a newer, bolder and more daring palette of bright, shocking electric blues and harmonizing shades of ultramarine blues. These are the colors of a peaceful sleep; consider using a blend of hues of the night sky, from twilight to a deep midnight blue, for a bedroom that calls for rest and relaxation.

Blue is known to slow down our heart rates and reduce anxiety in the way that red has the opposite effect. As the color of the ocean and the sky, blue provokes a slower rhythm and a more natural resting state than any of the hot, pulsating colors. For insomniacs or people with sleep disorders, a deep shade of blue is beneficial, whether it is used on the walls or for linens or both. Blue makes us think of truth and dependability, it creates a safe haven out of a bedroom even when used in the most daring applications.

Because blue is such a reliable color and standard favorite it gives designers the freedom to use it in more innovative and daring ways. Blue is a great background for giant murals and graphic textures. Use a brilliant indigo on a sofa or loveseat or as the background for a room furnished only in white.

↗
Equal parts vibrant blue and sun-bleached white. A wash made of cobalt pigment works harder than standard enamel paint to create the effect of a summer in Santarini in your bedroom. Add gauzy, white curtains to let in maximum sunlight to finish off the look.

↗
Blue and white bedding is a time-honored classic. Blue in a bedroom helps us feel calm and secure. Here a magnified ticking pattern blends with other variations on traditional bedroom patterns.

BLUE LOVES GOOD FOOD

Blue and white tableware has been a traditional part of almost every culture, from Egyptian pottery to Greek urns to Wedgwood and Flow Blue. Of course, tradition has a strong hold on styles and everything is bound to come back again at some point. Yet blue remains popular. Some suggest it is the best complement to food colors, others say that it has a beneficial effect on the diet. Either way, blue and white continue to return to the dining room in some form or another.

There are standard colors for dining rooms just as there are standard patterns for china, and there does seem to be a correlation. Slate blue walls are often seen with Jasperware china. Floral wallpaper will frequently match the blue and white china pattern. Cobalt glassware is teamed with chandeliers dripping with glass and crystals. But this is the old guard, and the kind of dining rooms we are now seeing are a more modern breed that are not afraid of a heavy dose of vivid color. Consider cobalt blue walls or a collection of cobalt glassware that takes up one entire wall. How about chandeliers or a tabletop made of blue glass? This may be a traditional color combination for the dining room but that only serves to give its bolder incarnation the staying power it needs.

Because of the varied trends in blue dining rooms, this color can span styles and periods effortlessly. For a nouveau-granny look, try using mismatched blue and white china against a bright sky background; add Philippe Starck chairs, and the look is complete. Many Asian-inspired designs use blue and white patterns that look just as at home with ornately carved cherrywood as they do with a vintage Saarinen tulip table. Whatever your preferences, using blue and white in the dining room is appropriate and, chances are, successful.

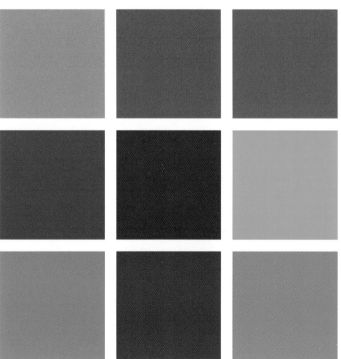

↑
Consider a new take on the classic blue and white by pairing white furniture and tableware against blue walls and a blue table. Modern bright blue makes the perfect contemporary background for a dining set in white plastic. Hardly the kind of plastics that we are used to, these latest incarnations are more fit for formal dining than a patio dinette.

↑
Whether you are planning to use a haughty peacock blue or a blaring electric blue or even one of the truer hues, blues have the largest universal appeal.

Any color that works in a dining room will work equally well for the kitchen. Striking blue works in both areas because it makes a brilliant backdrop for food. It sets a clean stage for fresh produce and steaming meals. Blue is also said to suppress the appetite so it could possibly be helpful to someone who is dieting, though it could also be a far stretch on the fad diet. Either way, bright blue is a tasteful way to decorate a kitchen that needs a lift. If you are too intimidated to lacquer the walls in a blazing cobalt, consider some of the new appliances that come in electric blue—from toasters to microwaves to electric mixers.

Another reason that kitchens shine when dressed in the color blue is that they go so well with standard kitchen surfaces. Electric blue and stainless steel make for a high-voltage professional-quality kitchen. The same goes for old-fashioned white enameled appliances and whitewashed country cabinets; bold blues are such a daring color that they will make almost any kitchen decor seem like a Pop-art design statement.

Lately, blue can be found in a selection of new surfacing materials from Corian to laminates that come in a wide array of bold colors and patterns. The textures of these new materials are well matched with pulsating shades of ultramarine. Shiny and slick, a warm-to-the-touch laminate looks like a reflecting pool. Combined with lots of mirrored surfaces, whether it is stainless in a kitchen or cool white porcelain in the bathroom, the shimmering qualities of electric blue synthetics are enhanced by other reflective surfaces.

→

Apart from the standard enamel, stainless, and white flooring, many kitchen elements are often green. When placed against an all-blue setting, these greens stand out beautifully. If you have a luscious view or large windows, electric blue is the perfect complement to leaf-green hues and shiny white complements.

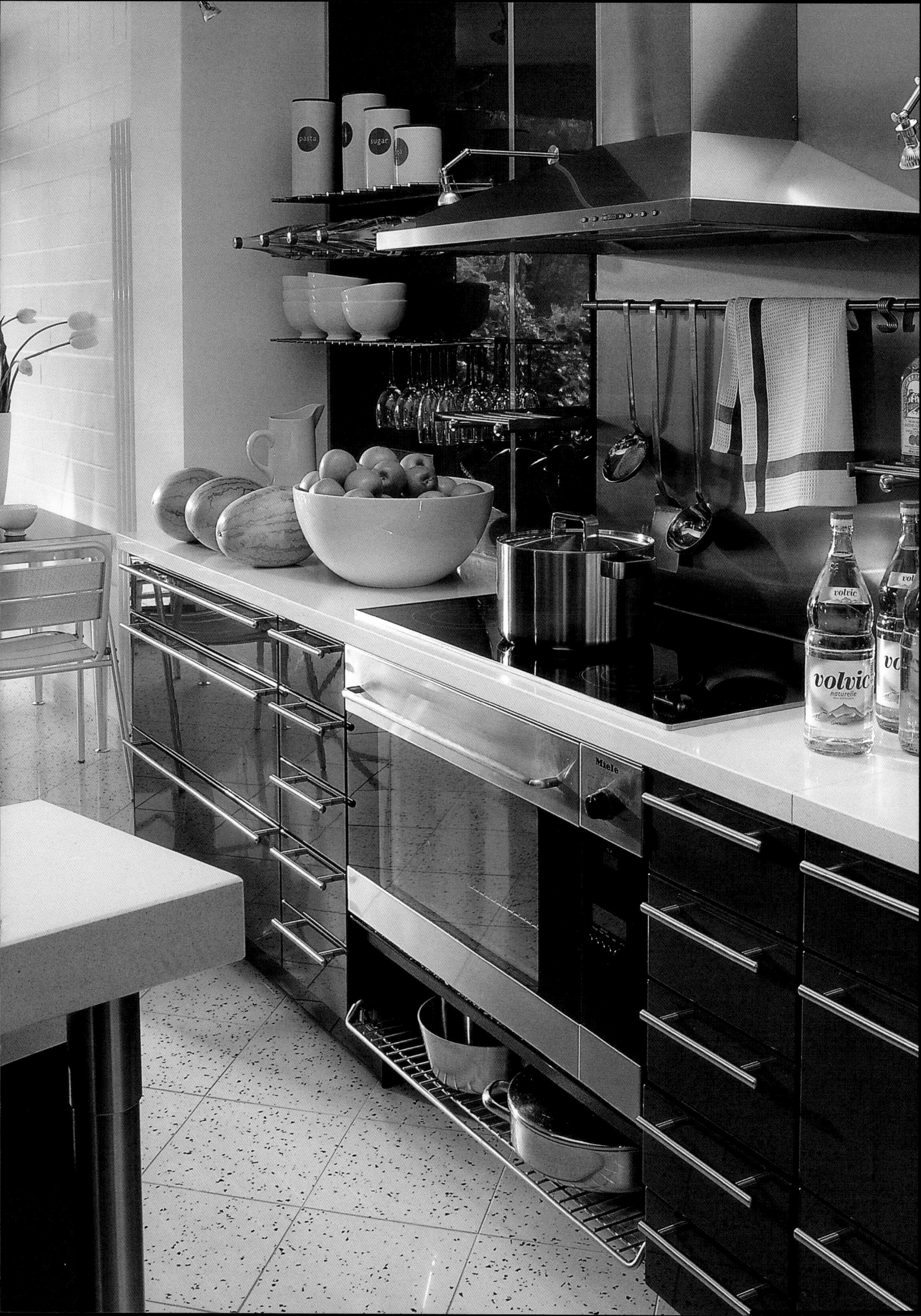
pasta
sugar
Miele
volvic
naturelle

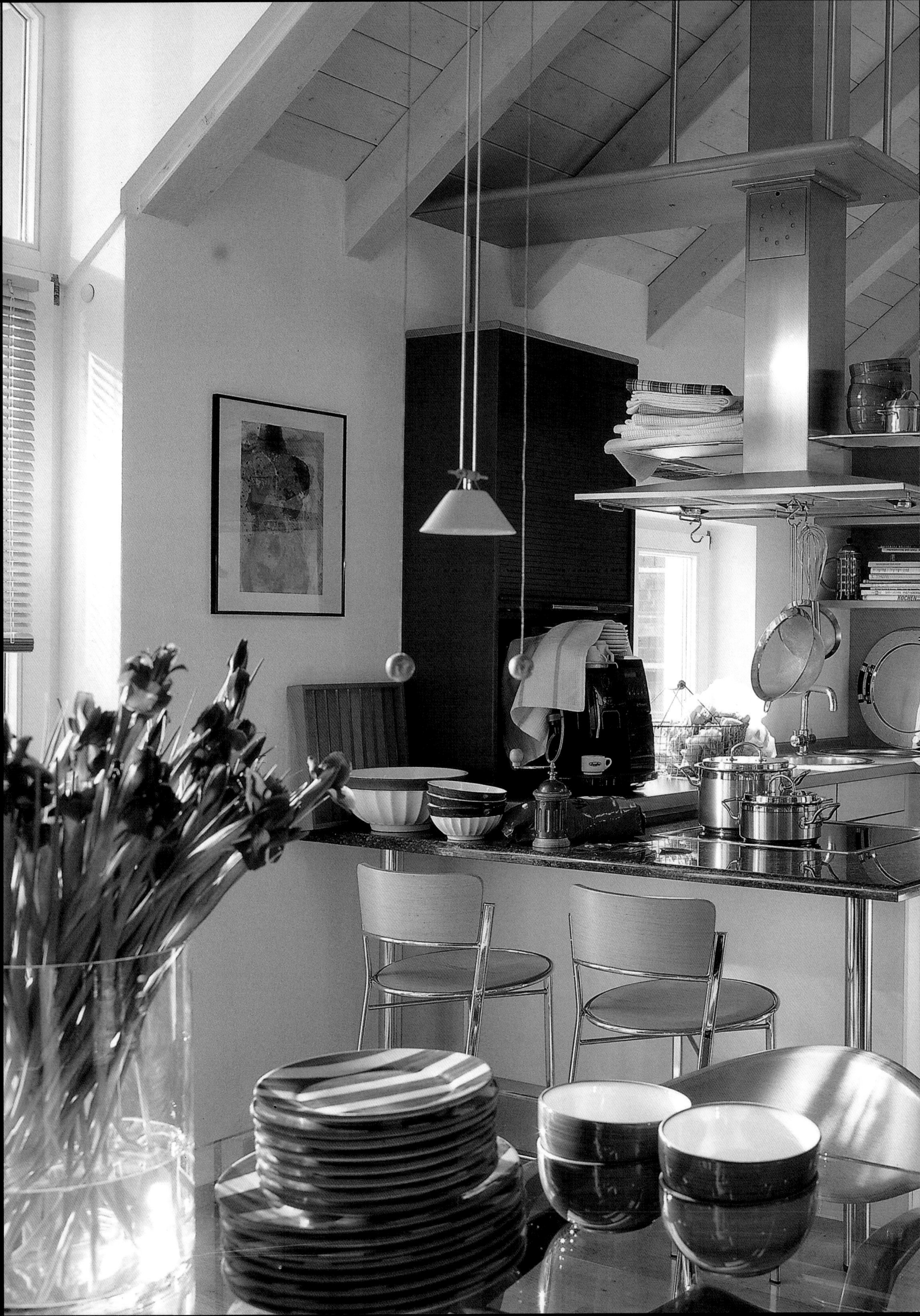

If your kitchen is too small, too cramped, or too difficult to maneuver in, blue is an excellent choice to remedy the situation. As a cool, receding color, it makes the living area larger, cooler, and more spacious. This can be a welcome illusion when you can't stand the heat from the oven, and there is more than one cook in the kitchen!

To take the illusion one step farther, try using pale, sky blue on the ceiling for an ephemeral effect. In cases where the ceiling feels too low, designers often use a pale whisper of blue to "push it up." This also seems appropriate as it imitates a blue sky overhead. Don't worry about the extant decor when painting a pale blue ceiling because the color of the sky will go with anything. If you are interested in using a color on the ceiling that is more daring, or if you want to wrap an electric wall color up and over the entire room, take care to add a few other colors to the mix. If not, the end result might feel a bit like you are drowning. Try using one shade lighter on the ceiling (if it's too deep, the ceiling will feel lower anyway) and adding generous touches of warm colors like yellow and orange.

As blue's complement, a caution-colored orange will make a brilliant blue even more memorable. Yellow has a similar effect because it, too, lies across from blue on the spectrum, though the combination is less striking and more harmonious than orange with blue. Yellow and blue seem to have a symbiotic relationship in that they mirror the sun against the sky. This successful duet works perfectly in a large, well-lit kitchen because it simply "feels" like a sunny day. If you are partial to intense blues, try adding a dash of equally intense yellow for a room that commands attention.

←
In a kitchen that combines architectural elements of galvanized steel and laminated birch wood, the interiors must match. Cold and warm, light and shadows; these contrasting moods are best highlighted by a decor of blue and yellow. Not only are the colors as powerful as the design, but they stand up to the architecture with their cheerfulness and vibrancy.

PEACOCK

FRENCH CUFF

INDIGO

DEEP END

SKY BLUE

STARRY NIGHT

ELECTRIC

MODERN GREENS

There are more shades of green than any other color in the spectrum. This hue can range in name from turquoise to forest to lime as it runs the gamut between yellow and blue. Think of the vast difference between racing green and sea-foam green, and you can begin to understand the expanse of hues that green encompasses. In its most vibrant shades, however, all green colors share the common benefits of looking fresh, energetic, clean, and easy.

In any variation, green is always the combination of warm yellow and cool blue; as a result it has a remarkable balancing effect anywhere you put it. Try using lime green in a kitchen that opens into a living room for easy entertaining and zesty cooking. Leafy greens will work wonders in a bedroom that longs for a calm color but runs from weak pastels. A shock of bold green in a neutral color scheme will instantly add a dose of fun without disturbing the relaxing vibe. Try using subtle persuasion with a "green-light means go" look for your home office or long, dreary corridor.

The range of greens is the most versatile of all the intense hues that we call bold colors because greens are a natural backdrop for wild color combinations and exotic palettes. Let yourself be inspired by a jungle scene that combines several shades of green with attention-grabbing touches of yellow, red, blue, and orange. The range of green is nature's equivalent to a neutral color scheme, so let go of all your fear and brush on the fresh, leafy hues and sea greens to create an energetic atmosphere that will feel like a vacation.

↑
Because yellow and blue make green, the combination of these three colors can't really go wrong. Slightly tweak each shade so that a primary yellow and a primary blue are mixed with an equally vibrant shade of green.

↖
Amply lit sitting rooms are the perfect place to use a bright leafy green. Paired with white trim and adjacent colors of blue and blue-green, the use of bold color is eye-catching but not startling. Green combined with blue makes for one of the most appealing combinations because it imitates the colors of the earth.

FACT FILE:

1. GREEN IS SAID TO BE THE MOST
   SOOTHING COLOR FOR OUR EYES
   SO USE IT IN YOUR HOME AS RELIEF
   FROM YOUR MULTI-HUED DECOR
   WITHOUT SACRIFICING FUN COLOR.

2. THINK OF THE WAY RED BLOSSOMS
   POP OUT FROM GREEN FOLIAGE,
   AND YOU WILL RECALL THE CON-
   TRASTING LESSON OF COMPLEMEN-
   TARY COLORS. USE THESE SHADES
   AS ACCENTS FOR EACH OTHER OR
   IN EQUAL MEASURES DEPENDING
   ON HOW YOU FEEL.

3. THERE ARE MORE VARIATIONS OF
   GREEN THAN ANY OTHER COLOR;
   MORE THAN 1,000 OF THE COUNT-
   LESS SHADES THAT OUR EYES REC-
   OGNIZE ARE CONSIDERED PART OF
   THE GREEN FAMILY.

4. LEAFY GREENS CAN BE USED AS
   FREELY AS A NEUTRAL BECAUSE THIS
   IS ESSENTIALLY, THEIR PURPOSE IN
   NATURE AS A PERMANENT BACK-
   DROP THAT NEVER SEEMS TO CLASH.

BRIGHT BLUE–GREEN IS MAGICAL

Blue-greens walk the line between earth and sky— they are both ephemeral and permanent, fantastic and grounding. And in their most vibrant potency, blue-greens can lend a magical touch. These blue-toned shades of sea-greens and turquoise blue are some of the most soothing colors in the rainbow. They are powerful when used as transitional shades for mixing blue and green and can be the perfect compromise if you can't decide which of these colors is right for you. Some of the cooler shades of green will act like a blue. Use a large dose of turquoise on a wall to make it recede and the entire room will seem larger. For an unexpected space-giving illusion, try wrapping a room in a daring blue-green shade of aquamarine. The effect will be less chilly than an icy shade of blue and infinitely more stylish. And, as adjacent shades on the spectrum, a vivid shade of blue-green will go harmoniously with accents of strong cobalt blue.

←
Teal green makes even this standard-issue entertainment unit look stylish and sleek.

← ↖
Even in its most shocking variations, green works well in a kitchen. Take care that a blue and green combination doesn't get too aquatic, though, or your food might taste a little saltier than usual. Here the combination works because the wood and neutral elements help bring the marine colors back to land.

← ←
As an accent color, lime green works hard to draw attention to itself. For a fabulous piece of furniture like this sofa, a daring shade of upholstery is a great way to keep it center stage. Fabrics with some sheen like raw silk or taffeta will enhance the vibrancy of zesty lime.

TEAL DRESSES UP ANY ROOM

Many of the blue-greens work hard to "dress up" a room with their gemlike and mystical associations. A high-sheen, topaz-colored paint or fabric can seem more formal than even gold or silver because of its luminescence. It is a color that we rarely see used in bold applications. Of course, teal and sea-foam green received their share of popularity in the 1980s when saturated fantasy colors were a logical reaction to the earth tones of the late 70s. Even though teal was overused in leather upholstery and as the "new" car color, it still makes a daring style statement for a large room or dramatic space. If you have a huge open space or a double-height great room, a coat of high-sheen teal paint will turn it into a place for special occasions.

We haven't seen much of these blue-green shades in several years, so now it seems like teal is the perfect choice when you want a mix of bold color and stylish nostalgia. Just be sure not to pair any of these colors with mauve or what could have been a magnificent throw back will seem more like you just never made it out of 1985. Instead, try combining teal with an adjacent shade of pine green or use it with lots of leafy foliage and a subtle splash of bright red or orange. For power-packed color in spaces reserved for entertaining, try pairing a bold blue-green with flaming magenta. When combined with warm woods and lots of lush greenery, the result is more comforting but slightly less fabulous.

Teal green works its charm best in spaces screaming for inspiration (and for designers looking for the same). Because it combines a saturated amount of blue and green, it is not a color that produces a standard response. Like purple, teal inspires us to dream. It's a great choice when you are stuck with a plain square of a room or inspired by magic-trick architecture like a floating staircase or slanting walls. It's the fantasy color of iridescent mermaids and thumb-sized fairies. Use this color in a monochromatic bedroom palette or for a formal dining room to call attention to your special china or 300 thread count bedding. It will twinkle in candlelight and glow under the sun or a skylight.

→
Teal green adds a dash of the exotic that looks stylish and sleek.

RESTFUL AQUA

For a calming and restful room that doesn't double as a sedative, consider greens with just a hint of blue like aqua or sea-green. These water colors are the perfect choice for a bathroom or a restful bedroom. They're also great colors to use poolside because they look right at home among tile, concrete, and blazing sunshine. Just think of the densely variegated swirls of color in the ocean. When using these colors, be sure to stick with your inspirational image and choose accents that match the theme. Both sun-bleached white and sandy beige will work well with these sea green shades. But don't eliminate the possibilities of brilliant sunshine yellows and dusk-dimmed fiery oranges.

The greatest thing about using water colors is that they are naturally at home in mottled or weathered applications that mimic the ocean. If you have walls that are stained or uneven, these shades will give them a sought-after look of variegated color. For a tiled bathroom, a collection of various blue and green one-inch tiles can come together for a reflecting pool look. There is also a wide array of special effects tiles and surfacing products on the market that use iridescent and textured finishes. These shimmery tiles can create the power of a desert mirage when used in turquoise, aqua, and sea foam green.

↑
The blue and green shades of sun-dappled water are used to their fullest potential as mosaic tiles in a bathroom. Instantly conjuring images of azure pools and topaz oceans, this combination works hard to transform a standard bathroom into a tropical paradise.

↑
Mixing blue-green with bright blue makes for an exotic jolt of color particularly when used in a silk brocade pattern or as upholstery. Consider making a pillow out of a silk scarf or blouse bought during a Mediterranean vacation, for a similar splash of color without the commitment.

GREEN THEMES

Green works well in a themed-motif because of its restful qualities. Consider a sea-inspired design with walls covered in iridescent wallpaper to look like water, a floor with a sandy-colored sisal and the decor matched to a nautical theme, complete with framed prints of sea turtles and turquoise leather seating. With shimmery walls and fresh, summer colors, even a tiny space can become a delightful retreat.

←

In any variation, green is always the combination of warm yellow and cool blue; as a result it has a remarkable balancing effect anywhere you put it.

Vibrant lime green is probably the farthest color from a neutral in the spectrum but it is beginning to feel as versatile as beige in this new millennium. It is shocking, invigorating, youthful, and yet, lime green can also be very restful and clean. It's like a natural neon, so use it in places where you want the freshening qualities of green without sacrificing eye-popping color and daring design.

For bathrooms and bedrooms, lime green should be used liberally but carefully. Designers frequently caution their clients about yellow-greens because they can sometimes get too acidic. However, as long as you temper the acidity of the color with some kind of "base" color, lime green can be used almost everywhere. In the bathroom, it's a good idea to match a zingy lime with some kind of powdery color or a creamy white. For bedrooms, make sure to keep a yellow-green fresh by combining it with lots of clean white. Sky blue will also serve to make these colors seem clean and fresh; consider using lime green on the ceiling or as small accents throughout a room.

Lime green makes a bedroom relaxing and daring. For people who love the outdoors, green can be as nurturing as a rosy pink or peach. Use it to create a bedroom sanctuary that is as soothing as pastel but not so insipid. Take care, however, that lime greens in the bedroom are not too yellow. Unlike pink and red, green is not known for its complexion-enhancing qualities. But, it is a fact that green is the most restful color for our eyes. In fact, the "green rooms" of backstage television were painted that color because of green's calming properties.

↖
In this bathroom, the unlikely combination of acid green with periwinkle blue creates an appropriate backdrop for a blend of vintage and industrial furnishings. The traditional purple-blue contrasts with a modern shade of green to match the contrasting colors of the furnishings and accessories.

←
Not only is green neutral enough to look great as a background for almost any color, but it also works naturally in a monochromatic scheme. Consider a meadow full of grasses or the produce aisle at the grocery; greens go together in any combination.

ENERGIZING HUE

Use the combination of yellow-green with blue-green to create the feeling of a tropical vacation in spaces that could use a dose of rest and relaxation like a home office or exercise room. These aren't the retired pastels of southern Florida or the washed-out palette of a soothing spa but rather the energizing colors of a new type of leisure that is fun, active, and creative. The magic of color association can be easily translated for use in the home; consider how quickly apple-green trimmed with a clean white would turn a musty attic into something fresh and tart. Let visions of the rain forest canopy be your newest inspiration by using a mottled assortment of succulent greens to turn your sunny exercise area into an invigorating space for self-improvement.

↗
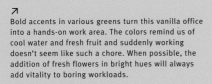
Bold accents in various greens turn this vanilla office into a hands-on work area. The colors remind us of cool water and fresh fruit and suddenly working doesn't seem like such a chore. When possible, the addition of fresh flowers in bright hues will always add vitality to boring workloads.

→
Studies have shown that while red promotes alertness and activity, green is the color that encourages you to follow through. In this home office, an innovative mix of vibrant lime green with aqua come together for an inspirational and soothing work space that promotes creativity and adds energy.

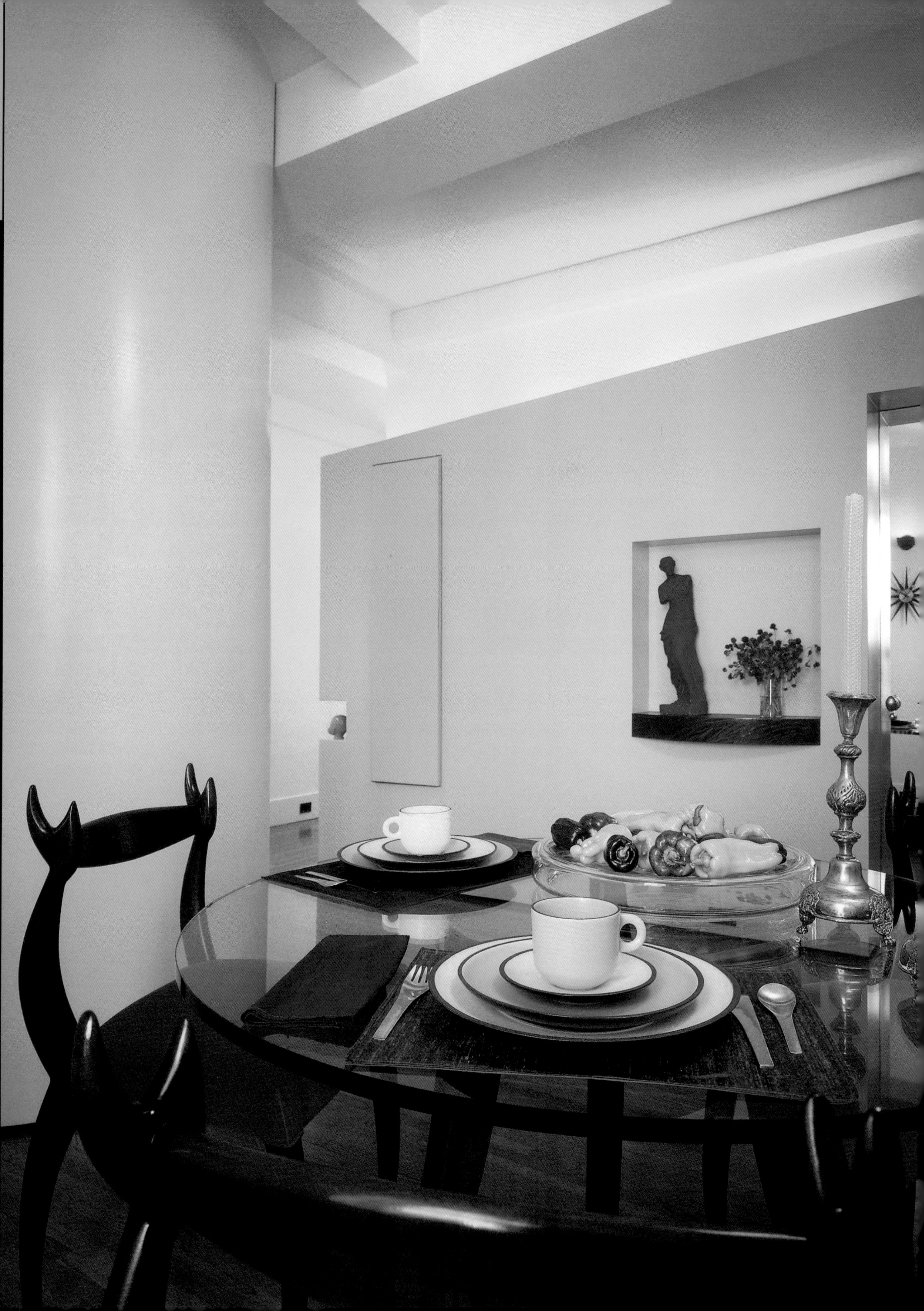

Lime green is a color that keeps coming back in vogue when something shocking is needed and in response to long periods of natural, neutral, and classic. Because it is none of the above, lime green is a stimulating choice for any room that needs a stylish face lift. If you are sick of your putty-colored sofa or khaki carpeting, lime green will be the antithesis. The Internet has exploited the "right now" properties of this color and it's being used as an advertising tool and logo standard. Home furnishings and accessories from chairs to lampshades are popping up in lime green and capturing everyone's attention.

Take a few precautions when bringing lime into the home. Remember that for bedrooms and bathrooms it might be best to pair lime green with soft powdery shades or sweetly scented floral colors to temper the tartness. In dining rooms and kitchens don't let yellow-greens get too slimy looking because it can tend to feel a little sickly. This doesn't mean that you have to tone down your preferred shade, but you should take the complementary colors and lighting into account whenever you are planning to use an acidic color in public spaces.

For dining rooms and living rooms that are reserved for entertaining, lighting must be carefully considered; Yellow-greens will look even more yellow when lit with warm light bulbs. Candlelight works with lime greens better than with any other shade of green, because of its yellow base. In a bedroom or bath where getting ready is part of the function of that space, yellow-greens should be well lit with bright white light or sunlight to keep the color true. One way to prevent green from casting a sickly wash is to pair the color with contrasting brights like hot pink or bold cobalt blue. The effect will make the green pop and break up the color so that it doesn't seem overwhelming.

↑
Red is the complement of green, so the combination of hot pink and lime green in this whimsical drawing room makes both colors stand out in contrast. Adding a trim of clean white to everything in the room prevents the space from feeling childish yet doesn't compromise the playful effect of the bright colors.

←
For dining rooms in lime green, take care that the lighting and color combinations counteract the tendency of green towards sickly hues. Here the pale yellow wash on one wall combined with cobalt accents team up to keep the green from looking artificial. The abundance of indirect subtle lighting allows for greater freedom and lighting combinations and effects.

LEAFY GREEN IS A NATURAL

As yellow-greens move closer to true greens and then into the darker shades, they run the gamut of natural foliage. Some of these bright leafy colors are the perfect way to add freshness in places where audacious colors may seem out of place. Vibrant and succulent greens are an easy compromise if you share your home with someone who doesn't care for pulsating color and wild decor. Green is a natural favorite, suggesting healthy plants or the shade of a giant tree. There are few people who dislike a vibrant, leafy green.

For areas like the kitchen or a breakfast nook, green's freshness factor creates a feeling of healthiness and vitality. Use any of the leafy greens in a kitchen, from lettuce greens to deep spinach; fresh foods and produce appear brighter. Avocado and olive greens are two retro favorites for the kitchen, though be sure to use these colors with bright shades of yellow, red, or orange so that the overall effect doesn't get too sallow. Shades of cucumber and apple green are subtler but work beautifully in a kitchen when paired with their flavor complements—tomato and red delicious apple.

Decorate the kitchen only with hues that seem to taste and smell appetizing. Pairing green with shades of blue or purple might cancel out some of the benefits by making it seem too cool or fishy. Instead, use green with bright doses of orange, yellow, or hot pink. Consider ceramic tile or some of the new surfacing materials for a contemporary look. Natural woods, used on butcher blocks and country farm tables, go inherently well with shades of green and the richness in both the wood grain and the color are highlighted when these elements are set together.

↑
In any variation, green is always the combination of warm yellow and cool blue; as a result it has a remarkable balancing effect anywhere you put it.

→
The surprising duet seen here pairs kelly green with a highly saturated hue the color of an artichoke. The effect is harmonious and the combination is unique enough to match the alternative dining environment, with industrial table offset by delicate orchids.

GREEN'S BALANCING ACT

↑
An innovative version of wainscoting breaks up a wall into two different shades. Here the contrast of pale pink with a true green creates the illusion of higher ceilings without sacrificing saturated color. This is also the perfect example of how well green works with dark woods like this mahogany desk.

True green, an even mixture of blue and yellow, lies smack in the center of the spectrum. Green, therefore, has a balancing effect on our bodies because it is neither warm nor cool. It does not advance to our eyes and increase temperature like red, yet it doesn't recede or cool like blue. Instead, green helps maintain our resting temperature and heart rate, and spaces seem approximately their true size. Green is the perfect color to use in a room that feels perfect except for it's lack of color; paint the walls with the equalizing hue and you've got color without spatial interference.

Green, being nature's neutral, is a good choice for living rooms and public spaces that entire families use. Consider green for cluttered spaces or rooms that can't avoid getting messy. There are few colors and textures that green doesn't look handsome alongside. It is an intrinsic background color, and even the most vivid greens won't disrupt the harmony of a room. But they will stand out; consider a monochromatic effect with the brightest, most saturated shade on the walls and everything else a deep or pale variation on that color. Another way to make green stand out is to add some complementary red to the mix, whether it is in the form of attention-grabbing artwork or one single throw pillow.

→
While it is a wild color, lime green can also be very restful, clean, and fresh looking.

TURQUOISE

CHILLY WATER

SWIRLING SEA

GEMSTONE

EMERALD

KELLY GREEN

LEAFY

ZESTY LIME

DARKER GREENS

It's easy to envision the rich green dress Scarlet O'Hara made from velvet drapes to visit Rhett Butler in *Gone With the Wind*. Darker shades of green—jade, pine, and emerald—have been around for centuries but that doesn't mean that there isn't a new, modern way to re-visit jade-colored dining and drawing rooms. Try adding contrasting touches of lavender with amethyst glassware or a colored-glass chandelier.

The first way to rethink the drawing room aesthetic is to pare it way down. Dark, vibrant greens are often used in about six different textures and varieties interrupted with lots of ornate gilding and chandeliers. For a contemporary look that feels sleek and clean, reinvent green by using it in one, expansive application. Consider painting a focal wall in a daring shade of green, or try it on the ceiling matched with honeyed hardwood floors. Thankfully, green doesn't play too many tricks on our eyes, so you can use it in various depth-defying ways—try it on every surface of a set of shelving or on a fireplace surround. For oddly shaped rooms, wrapping the whole space in green might be the perfect normalizing solution.

In more formal spaces, dark greens always look dapper. Combined with any type of wood, from mahogany to pine, green stands up to the test. Large polished estate pieces combined with green walls don't have to look traditional. Use a blaring green-light color rather than spruce to add a little kick. Pair old pieces with new, modern with classic, high furnishings with a low settee or try accenting green with polished aluminum rather than the classic match with ornate gilded frames. The possibilities are endless, but green can pull it all together because everything old and tired can easily be new again with a little imagination.

←
Vibrant and succulent greens are the perfect compromise if you share your home with someone who doesn't care for pulsating color and wild decor.

MIX IT UP

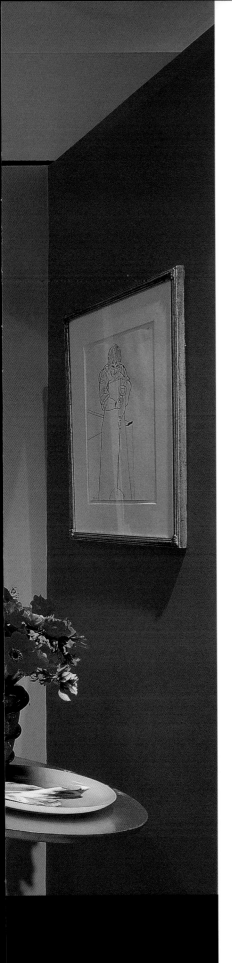

Now that you have learned everything you ever wanted to know about the palette of bright colors, how do you to use them all together. Creating a bold look with a combination of several vibrant colors is easy. However, keeping the overall effect clean, simple, and modern-looking is the hard part. As trends move away from the highly decorative and overly ornamental styles of traditional design towards a sleeker, more minimalist approach, we experiment with small doses of brilliant color—a single focal wall in blazing blue or a lime green staircase. But lately these starring colors seem to have had their day, making way for a wilder, louder approach to color. We have seen the techno-vivid hues of this millennium and now its time to mix them up a bit.

There is no incorrect way to mix color, though some combinations are more eye-catching than others. For the most daring look, pair brights of equal intensity and saturation together. Next to pastels, most vibrant colors overpower a room and stand out awkwardly in contrast. If you want lots of color without a pounding intensity, choose cooler shades or try adding relieving doses of white, black, or gray. Wild colors love the company of their peers, but they can also sing a beautiful solo when paired with pure white or up against a shiny black background. (Never use matte black because it absorbs most light around it, leaving little to be reflected by luminous color.)

Finally, never forget that there are no steadfast rules for combining the brightest colors in the palette. This chapter will take you through the various theoretical ways to combine colors but think of it, merely, as a set of reference points. Someone who prefers magenta to mauve isn't one to worry that it might clash against another hot hue like violet or bright orange. Brights are the signature colors of people who don't pay attention to traditional rules of decorating; they choose to create their own highly dramatic signature style. So, let go of everything you have ever heard about color combinations and go with what you like.

↖
This urban apartment easily parrots a bungalow in the tropics with the combination of five vibrant shades and lots of halogen spotlights. The effect of the lights bouncing off the colored walls and crossbeams not only accentuates the interesting architecture but turns this little apartment into an optimistic take on city living.

FACT FILE:

1. COMPLEMENTARY COLORS OPPOSE
   EACH OTHER ON THE SPECTRUM
   AND WHEN USED IN EQUAL INTEN-
   SITY AND PROPORTION, MAKE EACH
   ONE APPEAR BRIGHTER.

2. CONTRASTING COLORS INCLUDE
   COMPLEMENTARY COLORS BUT
   ALSO ANYTHING THAT ISN'T PART
   OF THE SAME FAMILY OF WARMS
   AND COOLS.

3. ADJACENT COLORS LIE NEXT TO
   EACH OTHER ON THE SPECTRUM,
   LIKE RED AND ORANGE, AND
   ALWAYS PAIR UP HARMONIOUSLY.

4. A TRIAD OF COLORS IS THREE HUES
   THAT ARE EQUAL DISTANCES FROM
   EACH OTHER LIKE THE PRIMARIES:
   RED, BLUE, AND YELLOW.

5. DON'T FORGET ABOUT BLACK AND
   WHITE WHEN PLANNING A COLOR
   SCHEME; THEY'RE NOT CONSIDERED
   COLORS BUT CAN BE IMPORTANT
   ELEMENTS WHEN COMBINING
   BRIGHTS.

EVERY COLOR IN THE RAINBOW

The wildest color schemes are ones that don't follow any of the suggestions in this chapter. Instead, the boldest, most daring looks are created from atonal color combinations and unrehearsed palettes. If this is the look you are going for, you can find inspiration anywhere and everywhere. Think of a field of wild-flowers with copper-colored columbine, fuchsia, aster, daisies, and lavender. Picture a sea of tropical fish among vibrant corals and kelps. Imagine a bowl of jellybeans or a box of Popsicles. There are no wrong choices if you simply want color and lots of it.

It's always nice to have one or two dominant colors in these kinds of interiors but I know how it gets when you want to see more of that lime green trim, say, on a pair of matching wing chairs? Color can become a powerful obsession and people who love it are prone to getting carried away, but it's really not such a dangerous obsession to have because color never causes permanent damage. Go ahead and paint your walls in seven different shades of green, if it's not what you pictured, you can always paint over it. The same goes for wallpaper, fabric, and small accessories that can quickly be peeled, stripped, or decoupaged and given another life in another shade. Color is either a temporary problem or a permanent pleasure, so you really can't lose, either way.

←
A multi-hued room is the perfect complement to an expansive collection of books, records, movies, or knickknacks. Only a monochromatic collection like green glass needs a subtle backdrop. Most collectors relish the mis-matched colors and covers of their most prized possessions; these kind of mis-matched decors dripping with every color go with the theme beautifully.

← ↖
Color washing is one of the best ways to create an authentic tropical color palette. Here classic pigments are used to create seven saturated shades of wash that are applied coat after coat until a desired mix of uneven colors are reached and the effect meets that of an island outpost.

← ←
The shades used in this screen are the perfect example of an adjacent color scheme. Hot hues of red, pink, orange, yellow, and lime green are illuminated and serve as a glowing backdrop for a sexy red sofa.

COMPLEMENTARY COLOR SCHEMES

Orange and blue—the coolest and the hottest shades in the spectrum—come together for the boldest combination of complementary hues. Designers have varied opinions about how to deal with such colors that lie on opposite sides of the color wheel. Some believe that the contrast can be too much, suggesting only small doses of a complement, like yellow flowers in a purple bathroom. Traditional design has discouraged the use of complementary colors in the brightest hues and offers a variation on this scheme that suggests matching hunter green with rose rather than a true green with bright red. But the boldest color schemes take advantage of the impression made by starkly contrasting colors: blue with orange, red and green, purple plus yellow, all compete for the most eye-catching combinations.

Complementary colors are not restricted to the six main hues. For equally competitive color duets, try pairing a cool turquoise with a fiery coral or a hot magenta with a tangy lime green. Don't be afraid to team up these unlikely combinations but be aware that these matches make a powerful pair. Feel free to use them equally, but do add some elements of relief like pure white or a temperate shade of gray. Part of the reason that complementary colors can be so overwhelming is due to the principle of "after-image," which means that if you stare at a red sign for long enough, when you look away, you will see an after-image of green.

The wrong action to take against complements that feel too competitive is to water down one of your bold colors. The combination of pale peach with a blazing cobalt blue will only make your decor seem asymmetrical. Pairing a pulsating color next to a pastel version of its complement seems an insult. Instead use each color in small doses with plenty of "white space" and gradually add more color until it feels wild but naturally harmonious. Playing around with floral arrangements is always a good way to get an idea of which color combinations suit you.

↑
The duo of orange and blue is one of the most
vibrant color combinations because it matches the
hottest color in the spectrum with the coolest, in
equal intensities. Each color enhances the other,
making them both stand out in pulsating contrast.

OTHER TYPES OF CONTRAST

Complementary colors are not the only matches that make color sing out. Whether you are using two colors or ten, any match up of shades that are not "adjacent" on the color wheel, are considered contrasting. This means warm colors combined with cools, greens with orange, or a bright purple paired with leafy green. Decorating with contrasting colors is always a daring way to go.

For inspiration in creating contrasting color palettes, think first to some of your favorite colors from childhood. I always remember my dual-tipped colored pencils and how the hot pink and sky blue was my favorite. To this day, this is still one of the color combinations I use and wear most frequently. If you don't have specific memories of your art supplies or visions of Aunt Edna's Fiestaware collection, then you can take some of the principles of color theory and make them your own. For instance, the theory of "split complements" suggests the harmony of a color with the two shades on either side of its complement. Try this by using bright orange with a blue-green and a blue-purple for a harmonious two-tone scheme.

You can also alter the rule of complements by shifting the colors in whichever direction you choose, like red with bright aqua or canary yellow with fuchsia. For an even wilder look, try using more than one pair. Pair up two adjacent colors with their opposing shades for twice the contrast. This is also a great way to prevent your look from getting too matched. Incorporating variations on your star colors is a great way to add depth to a color scheme. Consider a bathroom done in cool blue tile with vibrant orange accents on the shower curtain, bath mat, and light fixture; adding some tangerine-colored candles and hand towels will add an extra layer of bright color.

↑
The boldest color schemes take advantage of the impression made by starkly contrasting colors: blue with orange, red and green, purple plus yellow, all compete for the most eye-catching combinations.

↑
This contrasting color scheme presents the three cool colors in vivid concentration set off by a warm yellow-orange on the ceiling. Here the wild colors play up the architectural details of a room with alternating wall depths.

←
A strong combination of lime green and deep coral offer a wild take on contrasting colors by adding yellow to the complementary shades of red and green. Feel free to pair any contrasting colors that you like, as long as they are of equal brightness.

TRIADS ADD THREE TIMES THE PUNCH

PRIMARY COLORS

The combination of the three primary colors—red, yellow and blue—sets the stage for pure color drama. These three colors are the basis for all other colors and each one stands boldly and confidently on their own without any help from the others. Together, they form the most elementary of triads. Unfortunately, many people tend to associate the primaries with children's toys but combining yellow, blue, and red can make a mature, graphic statement. Think of the designs of Gerrit Rietveld, the paintings of Piet Mondrian, and Yves Saint Laurent dresses inspired by Mondrian's "perfect grid." They are inspiration not only for a nursery but also for wild living spaces.

Consider creating a basic bold bedroom using equal parts of red, blue, and yellow or a series of adjoining rooms in a monochromatic scheme of each. The amazing effect of this combination occurs when light is reflected off these adjoining colors. Don't forget that color is essentially a reflection of light; consider that when a red wall is reflected onto a yellow, it casts an orange tone, and when a yellow wall reflects the blue, it creates a green glow. Depending on the amount of light entering a room, the effect could be like a prism. Try testing this theory by installing high-sheen laminates, in each of the primaries, for a kitchen or bathroom that mimics a rainbow when the light pours in.

An entirely different look would be to keep each primary surrounded by blocks of white, black, or gray. By locking these colors in their own space, you will preserve the constancy of the color. This is what Mondrian was doing when he colored geometric shapes of bold primary color inside a grid of black on white.

↑
Here the combination of red, blue, and yellow is presented as a Mondrian-inspired bathroom done entirely in laminates. This color scheme has the tendency to feel cold and austere, so the use of warm-to-the-touch laminate is a good solution for a bold yet cozy bath.

↑
Blue, yellow, and red are the three primary colors and the basis for all bolds and brights. Pairing them together in equal parts creates a graphic illusion for any applications, but in geometric shapes and large patterns, these colors come alive.

LIME GREEN, RASPBERRY, AND VIOLET

For an explosion of color that is less expected than the triad of primaries, try teaming up three vigorous shades of pink, blue, and green. Mixing warm with cool colors is always a good rule for creating a bold space that is memorable for its wild color combo rather than the way it affects anyone who enters. These types of color schemes are audacious and not as affecting as an entirely warm or cool palette.

Designers often use a three-color scheme to call attention to architectural details because painting asymmetrical spaces in contrasting colors can highlight unusual design features. The same kind of theory can be used for a room that is lacking architectural interest. Simply by using three bright colors for various aspects of the room, you can create the illusion of depth and spatial irregularities.

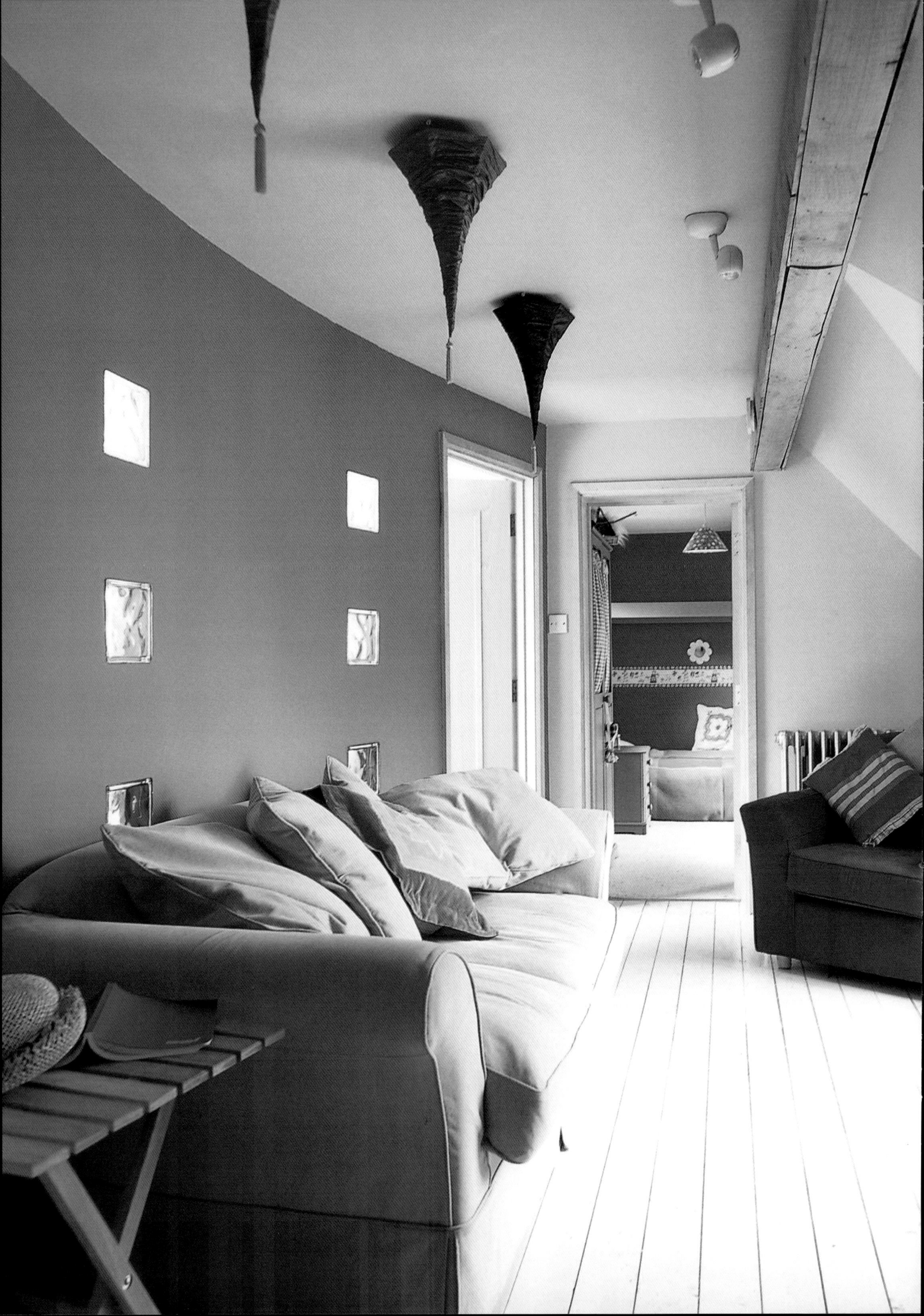

ADJACENT WARM COLORS

↑
A sweet shade of orange is cooled off by a bit of green and freshened with a dash of yellow.

←
Adjacent colors, orange and yellow, combine for a sunny room that isn't overwhelming due to the expanse of white and neutral elements.

With the recent popularity of Eastern-inspired textiles and patterns, we have begun to see more warm-hued palettes that focus on spicy oranges, bright pinks, and deep reds. Imagine the feeling of walking into a room drenched with the most vibrant shades of pink, yellow, and orange. Forget about the daisy patterns and flame stitch patterns emblazoned on these colors in the 1970's; instead think of huge expanses of saturated color and big graphic patterns using warm hues in near-neon shades. Color combinations, like this, that mix shades next to each other on the spectrum, are referred to as "adjacent." Wrapping a room in any or all of the hot brights or cool colors is the fastest way to spice up a room and make it unabashedly stylish at the same time.

When picking out shades for a warm-sided color palette remember that reds and orange are the hottest shades with yellow and pink right behind them. For a glowing effect that doesn't get too steamy try mixing red with yellow or orange with pink rather than orange with red. Of course, if that is your plan then go for it; but be careful to throw in some neutral sage green or warm-toned white. Whatever colors you choose, be sure to pair these warm colors in equal intensities so that one shade doesn't swallow up another.

Decorating with adjacent colors does not require you to use the shades in an order that corresponds to their place in the spectrum nor does it restrict to the standard shades. Feel free to place red next to yellow and orange next to pink; it's the warmth and luminescence of these colors that make them harmonious not the fact that they are sisters on the color wheel. The same goes for the cool side of the wheel. Any combination of green, blue, and purple will blend beautifully and create a calm, cooling atmosphere but feel free to mix it up with borderline cools like key lime or magenta.

TROPICAL HUES

Tropical color palettes are perfect for rooms that get lots of light or are in warm climates, but don't let that discourage you from using these colors anywhere from a Boston high-rise to a Cotswold cottage. The lime greens, vibrant yellows, pinks, and cheery reds work so well in sunny atmospheres because they combine to create a breathtaking palette that suits warm weather and intense light. However, these colors can create an inspirational interior in places far removed from the actual tropics.

These are the colors of leisure and the palettes of regions where an upholstered settee is not as useful as a sun-baked hammock. These are shades to compete with the bluest skies and aquamarine beaches; and these hues have to be colorfast and weatherproof. Think of the color-washed plaster of Mexican casitas or the multi-colored huts on Bahamian beaches. These are not Miami pastels or L.A. neons, but a true tropical palette that mixes every color under the sun with little regard to tradition, trends, or taste. When selecting your tropical colors, try to put yourself in mind of warm lagoons and palm trees to capture the mood.

If you don't have huge windows or a 360-degree view, consider adding a lot of light to your color-drenched interior. This is not a decor to hide in the shadows of dim, dramatic lighting but rather a place to flood with light. Don't be afraid that the combination will be overly bright because saturated color is what this scheme is about. Use a different shade on every wall, or break up a wall into stripes or blocks of color. In short, combining approximately five or six tropical-hue shades in full-effect will work to turn any room into a beachside cabana.

CITRUS COLORS

Lemon yellow, lime green, and orange are the three zestiest colors, because they remind us of citrus scents and tangy flavors. Paired in combinations of two or three or in variations on the theme, these citrusy colors come together for a dazzling effect that will turn any room into a space with a refreshing twist. Bright citrus shades of yellow, green, and orange can be used in a variety of intensities from almost eye-popping fluorescent colors to spicier shades that still feel invigorating when shown with their counterparts. With these colors, you could opt for shades ranging from a deep mandarin orange to a pale lemon yellow and they will still appear to glow because of their inherent vibrancy. Each color contains undertones of yellow, the most luminous hue, so their reflective ability is unbeatable, and the trio of these colors only makes the effect that much brighter.

FAST FIXES

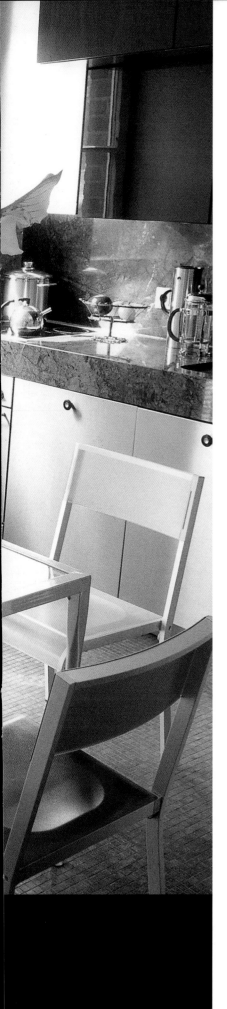

When deciding on which bold colors to use in your home, there are many factors to figure in. The first step is to keep your options strictly to colors that you love. Everyone has preferred colors, the shades they wear, the hues they are drawn to when asked to choose from the now ubiquitous rainbow of options. These are the colors to consider when picking bright colors for your home, because you'll be the one living with them. Bold, shocking expanses of color do not just exist as a background like neutrals; they practically jump off the walls to make their statement so you need to like what they have to say and love the way they look.

Don't forget to consider all the practicalities of your living space. Always be sure that your colors are appropriate for the function of the room. A lemony yellow kitchen will always be more appealing than a turquoise one because it suggests an appetizing flavor, just like a bedroom works best in soothing shades rather than a vibrant yellow that might contradict sleepiness. No one is exempt from the natural associations of colors, especially bright shades, so keep these in mind when matching up colors to specific rooms.

Remember to try out all colors before you start redecorating. Live with a test patch of paint on the wall for a couple weeks, drape a fabric sample over its future frame, lay a carpet sample on the floor and see how you like it. My mother was the master of this, and I can remember sitting on fabric that was pinned to the sofa for months before she decided it was suitable to be more permanently attached. Of course nothing in our home was ever permanent, but rather a constant flux of samples, replacements and endless accessories that either worked beautifully or were banished to Goodwill without a single regret. I try to remember this when I've made my own decorating miscalculations: Just about anything can be fixed, switched or instantly re-done in the quest for the perfect color scheme.

FOR BOLDER
AND BRIGHTER

The easiest color problem to fix is not having enough. Many people's dreams for a daring decor are daunted by outside factors. But whether it's a limited budget, restrictive leasing contracts, or a co-habitant who prefers sage to chartreuse, there are several stealthy ways to introduce bold color into your bland existence. And if your color choices were dulled by last-minute jitters or the ever-regretful color compromise, there are also a few easy ways to turn up the intensity without starting from scratch. Always remember that with color, it is easier to add than to subtract.

If your problem is a plain white box that you are renting only temporarily, try out a couple cheap and chic solutions for adding vibrancy to your lackluster decor. An easy project (which can also be transported from home to home) is curtains made from a bold, bright fabric like the colorful graphics of Marimekko textiles or remnants of a vintage 1950's Hawaiian print. For a larger investment, a multi-colored, geometric area rug will add warmth under foot and a base of color. Brightly upholstered furnishings teamed with eye-catching accessories, look hot up against pure white walls.

The first step in converting anti-color roommates is to get them used to vivid color by bringing home fresh cut flowers in a selection of bright shades. Slowly but surely you can add dashes of color with small accessories, working your way up to something more permanent like a sofa the color of a taxi cab. If you are suffering from the brownish result of the compromise between your tangerine dreams and your roomie's preference for an earthy terracotta, try adding a dose of the complementary color. Again start with something unassuming like a vase of irises to make the orange tones stand out in contrast to the blue. The easiest way to turn up the volume on color is to pair complementary colors together; and the more equal the proportions, the bolder the colors will appear.

If your colors still seem dull or tired, consider turning up the lights. Adding a spotlight is the fastest and most obvious solution to making colors sing out; pointed at a brightly painted wall, an intense light allows more color to be reflected. Finally, don't limit your favorite brights to the walls. Color can be added anywhere, from floors to ceilings, over windows and inside closets and on anything that can tolerate a coat of paint. In fact, it might be a good idea to keep a pint of your favorite paint color on hand for that flea market find that would be fabulous if only it was a little more colorful.

TO TONE
IT DOWN

Decorating with color takes practice and a trial-by-fire attitude so it is highly probable that you will end up, at some point, with a result that doesn't work. Whether it is too many colors or one single hue that feels unrelentless in its vibrancy, there are a few simple ways to tone down too much color. The first step is admitting that your bohemian-style living room, with its multi-colored patterns and loud colors, feels more like a circus tent than a den of inspiration. The next step is eliminating one or two of the overwhelming elements.

Color washing is an effective way to tone down too-bright color. Basically, it involves thinning regular paint with either water or a glazing compound for a translucent wash that can be applied over a base coat until the desired effect is achieved. Using a color wash with any of the countless combinations produces a deeper and more textured appearance than standard opaque paint. For colors that feel too bright, first consider washing over them with either a white-based wash that will take the edge off or a brown glaze for an instantly aged effect. Consider using a white color wash over cobalt blue to calm down a bold bedroom. A brown glaze over neon lime green will instantly age the color to a less artificial hue for a natural green porch swing.

Eliminating some of the contrast and competing patterns is another way to freshen up a room that is beginning to feel like a fun house. Try choosing one, less prominent color and replacing it with a clean white or a cool gray for added sophistication. In multi-colored rooms, there often needs to be a healthy dose of neutrals to provide relief for our color-stimulated eyes. Many shades of green will provide the same kind of eye-relief without sacrificing any of your color.

If your living room seems like it is ruled by dueling patterns, like the overly chintzed drawing rooms of the 1980s, try throwing a natural canvas slipcover over one or more upholstered pieces. Next time, opt for one or two bold patterns in blazing color over several tiny prints. If your Indian dhuri or Oriental rug is clashing with your simple color scheme, move it into an entryway and replace with an equally exotic white or beige Flokati rug. The same goes for artwork in a room that is overwhelmed with color; switch the Kandinsky in the bright orange dining room with the black-and-white photos from your yellow bedroom. After adding neutrals and covering some of the offending patterns, if your room still feels more vulgar than visionary, try turning down the lights. In a room bursting with color, always use indirect task lighting rather than a blinding overhead lamp. If overhead is your only option, try installing a dimmer to lower the light on a room bursting with color.

UNEXPECTED RESULTS ARE EASY TO FIX

Often times, people will complain to designers that their paint color didn't turn out as expected. When looking at tiny, little squares of paint chips it is extremely difficult to visualize how the shade will look over an entire room, not to mention in relation to furniture and lighting. Don't forget that in practical applications, color never exists alone as it does on a 1-inch square paint sample. The best way to test drive a color is to buy a pint before investing in a larger quantity and paint either a 2-foot patch directly on the wall or on a piece of poster board to lean against the wall. Seeing the color vertically against the wall will help you gauge how it will look in both day and evening light and combined with other colors in the room.

If your color is not at all how you imagined, there are a couple ways to quickly fix this without starting from scratch. Before you decide to re-paint your walls with the requisite three to four coats for coverage, try to come up with a quicker solution that relies only on a basic knowledge of color mixing. (If you don't trust your finger-painting memories you can always practice with toy store craft paints and watercolors.) Keep in mind that color interaction, as well as lighting, will affect our perception of the shade. Consider a hot pink wall; on the sample it may have seemed vibrant and daring but in relation to your red leather Barcelona lounge, it seems a bit weak. For a quick fix, add some accents of lime green or white to draw out the color. In contrast to its complement or a tone that is drastically lighter, most colors will sing out. If you had imagined the shade as warmer or

cooler, pair it with a color that implies these properties. Hot pink next to orange will seem warmer, while a deep indigo will bring out the blue undertones. Alternately, you can try different lighting levels and light sources to see which will bring out the desired appearance.

One thing to remember about this kind of color interaction is that our perception of the color is changing, not the color itself. If you can't be fooled by the sensation of warmth with the addition of some red pillows or incandescent lighting, it may take a more measurable effort. Color washing is a good way to slightly alter paint colors that are not working. Darken or lighten colors with tints of white wash or a veil of black-based wash. For warmer hues, add a translucent yellow color wash over the existing paint. For cooler colors try adding a blue wash but be careful not to wash a color with its complement or you will get a muddied effect.

For paints that don't work because the finish is all wrong, there are glazes and clear coats in every gloss level. High-gloss lacquer paints can be overwhelming at times. When done correctly, red lacquer on kitchen cabinets can look like a racecar but on surfaces that aren't slick like rough plaster, shiny surfaces only call attention to the imperfections. Glossy paint can also be too reflective and cause eyestrain in areas with lots of light. Before starting over, try coating these surfaces with an eggshell glaze, though some sanding may be required depending on the kind of lacquer used. The reverse steps can also be taken to add sheen to an overly matte finish that makes bright colors seem dull and lackluster. If none of these options seems appropriate, there is always the possibility of starting over; with so many boldly bright shades of paint, it seems a shame to live with a color you don't love.

TURN UP
THE HEAT

Many times the effect of an entire color scheme ends up being the opposite of what was expected. Of course much of these temperature problems are due to climate conditions; in sunny California a cool place to retreat and watch movies might be the perfect place but in gray climates like Seattle or London, a cool colored decor will only exacerbate the rainy-day blues. Always keep climate and lighting in mind when choosing colors.

The easiest way to fix a temperature problem is to add a few accents of warmth. For a bathroom wrapped entirely in icy blue tiles, the addition of white accents will only make the room feel frostier. Instead, resist the urge to maintain the cool palette and add a soft, fluffy bathmat in flaming orange or sunshine yellow. Too much chrome and glass can also enhance a cold feeling; replace sleek chrome fixtures with warm translucent plastic in pink or red. This can also be a problem for kitchens that combine blue tile with white marble, stainless steel or cold enamel; in this case a single vase of bright flowers will instantly turn up the heat.

Cool color combinations will not only make rooms appear about six to seven degrees colder but will also make the dimensions of the room seem larger. These problems can quickly be countered with a warm-toned color wash. For blues and greens, a wash of warm yellow will steer the color towards a warmer shade of green. For deeper blues and purples, a wash of pink or red glaze can create a temperate shade of lavender or warm magenta, depending on how many layers you apply. As long as your wash color is harmonious to the base color, you can paint on as many layers as necessary to achieve the perfect color concentration.

In large rooms, there are additional color wash techniques that can be used to make the space appear smaller. When used over bold colors, these shading or fade-away washes will add some interest to the colors while manipulating the spatial appearance. Two shades of red glaze over bright blue paint, with the dark red glaze melding into the lighter red about halfway up the wall, will create a variegated purple color that makes the ceiling appear higher; reverse the effect to lower the ceiling by using the darker shade near the top of wall (and over the entire ceiling, if that is blue, too.) If this isn't a fast enough fix, you can always make a room feel smaller, turning up the heat simultaneously, with a room divider or screen in a hot shade of flaming red, orange, or gold.

TURN UP THE A/C

Finding yourself in a room that feels hot and claustrophobic is more common than the reverse effect. Red and orange have a powerful effect on us physiologically, which only makes their unrelenting presence in a space that much more overwhelming. As most warm colors are advancing, we might find that a room decorated all in red makes us feel closed in and agitated. If you love a vibrant red, this won't be as apparent but for many people too many warm brights can cause their pulse to race and their body temperature to rise.

As we have learned, there are many easy ways to turn down the heat with other cool colors, fresh whites and an open window, but subtracting warmth is one of the more difficult color tricks. For too much red or yellow, the simple solution is to add a cool variation on these colors. Purple flowers or indigo pillows can quickly temper a blazing red love seat and a burning yellow can be cooled with a translucent blue wash to produce a fresh shade of green. But with many shades of orange turning down the heat becomes a little more difficult. Adding accents of blue might counter the temperature a bit but will also be sure to make the orange stand out stronger than before. Any attempt to color wash orange with a cooler shade will turn the color into a muddy brown.

The only way to cool down the color orange is to wash it with white color wash for a lime washed apricot look. At the risk of losing some of the ferociousness of a daring color scheme, a whitewash will immediately temper any hot color by turning it into a milky version of its former self. In order to keep the bold color while freshening up the feel, consider adding a greater proportion of white, cream, or a pale whisper of green. Window trim and crown molding are good places to use white, but you can also increase its presence by using it from the floor to dado height. A pastel variation of sky blue on the ceiling will add a cooling touch overhead, if your shocking pink bedroom suddenly makes you flushed and feverish. Adding white in the form of a fuzzy rug or window sheers will also help turn down the heat.

COUNTERING YELLOW-GREEN UNDERTONES

In some cases it isn't the color that causes the problem but the situation where it's used. You may absolutely love the shade of chartreuse that you chose for your bathroom but you can't help being slightly disgusted at the way it makes your skin look sallow while you're brushing your teeth. To counter some of the yellow-green undertones, you could coat it with a few layers of sea green color wash or a basic white wash. Another option would be to keep the color to the lower half of the room, on the walls up to waist height and on the floors, so that the color isn't level with your face when looking in the mirror. There are many cases where the chosen color was a good idea and it looked great until you attempted to carry out the functions in that space.

Bedrooms and bathrooms are areas that should use colors that are complexion-enhancing and soothing, although the latter is up to interpretation. Kitchens and dining rooms work best in appealing colors and living rooms or spaces reserved for entertaining are always nice in the most vibrant and energetic hues. If you have come to the realization that your color choices are not the best match for your rooms, there are always a couple easy options to attempt before renovating the entire decor.

As we've mentioned throughout this chapter, the easiest way to alter the perception of colors is to match them up with different ones. For a deep blue narrow hallway that's a drag to walk through, hang a brilliant yellow painting on the wall (you can also paint the ceiling and floor in a darker hue to make the corridor appear wider) and it will add a jolt of high-voltage energy. An overly opulent red and purple boudoir can be toned down for a more modern twist on sexy by adding pale pink and white to let out some of the steam. Similarly a kitchen done in insipid pastels of yellow and green is hardly reminiscent of hearty meals; add wild splashes of bright citrus hues to increase the appetite and turn up the volume.

DON'T BE AFRAID

There are a hundred ways to fix a color palette that seems to have taken a wrong turn along the way—this is the most important color lesson to remember. No color or color combination is permanent; there is always a can of something to cover up a bad decision or overexcited vision. So the final problem to correct is the fear of color being too much. Unlike the minimalist, industrial-gray-loving anti-colorist, the problem of color shyness has a simple solution: Get over it!

The number one reason to not be afraid of decorating with bold, bright color is that it is a guaranteed mood lifter. The second reason not to be timid is that the statement made by a brightly colored interior is one that is daring and unforgettable. And finally, if you hate it, you can always change it. But, if you love these colors—love wearing them, photographing them, or planting them—the chances are you won't hate living with them. If your fears are still there, then start small and work your way from room to room; instead of wrapping a room in brilliant turquoise, color one wall at a time and add accents bit by bit.

Finally, be sure to pick colors that you love and are used to. If you never wear red and think it looks bad on you, certainly don't paint your bedroom that color. By choosing colors that you wear or carry or accessorize with, you will insure that the decor matches your personality and makes you feel good. It's your home—why would you care what anyone else thinks of your color choices? Be bold, be brave and you'll show your real colors!

BOLD COLOR PALETTES

Bold Yellows

CITY SLICKER

RUBBER DUCKY

TAXI CAB

LEMON DROP

YELLOW ZEST

JUICY

DAFFODIL

SUNFLOWER

Wild Oranges

SORBET

TANGERINE

LOLLIPOP

PAPAYA

RAW SILK

PUMPKIN

MANDARIN ORANGE

Racy Reds

CRIMSON KISS

CINNABAR

SCARLET

HOT PANTS

LIPSTICK

RITZY RED

CHINESE POPPY

VERMILION

RACECAR RED

Shocking Pink & Purple

BUBBLEGUM

BLUSHING

FUCHSIA

RASPBERRY

SIZZLING PINK

AUBERGINE

LILAC

GRAPE POPSICLE

LIZ'S LOOK

Cool Blues

PEACOCK

FRENCH CUFF

INDIGO

DEEP END

SKY BLUE

STARRY NIGHT

ELECTRIC

Modern Greens

TURQUOISE

CHILLY WATER

SWIRLING SEA

GEMSTONE

EMERALD

KELLY GREEN

LEAFY

ZESTY LIME

DIRECTORY/PHOTO CREDITS

Abode UK, 13 (top); 28 (top); 31; 104 bottom; 114; 128 (bottom)

Bernard O'Sullivan/Abode UK, 48; 80; 133 (bottom)

Ian Parry/Abode UK, 13 (bottom); 25 (top); 38; 78; 86 (bottom); 113; 129 (bottom); 131; 139 (bottom)

Trevor Richards/Adobe UK, 86 (top); 100 (top)

Simon Whitmore/Abode UK, 104 (top); 139 (top)

Alexander Julian at Home, 98

Antoine Bootz, 24 (bottom); 35; 63; 67; 117; 132 (bottom); 133 (top); 134 (top)

Art Gray, 85

©Bathroom décor by Sarie/Camera Press, 37

Grey Crawford/Beateworks, 5; 16 (top & bottom); 21; 24 (middle); 81; 84 (bottom); 112; 123 (bottom)

Tim Street-Porter/Beateworks, 29; 40; 57; 66 (top); 118 (top); 132 (middle); 135

Courtesy of The Glidden Company, 3 (bottom); 20 (bottom); 59; 64; 82

Courtesy of Ikea 2001, 3 (top and middle); 58; 70; 101

Dupont Corian, 15; 53; 124 (top); 136 (top)

Dupont Zodiaq, 54 (top); 89

Nadia MacKenzie/TheInterior Archive, 55 (top)

Simon Upton/The Interior Archive, 90

Fritz von der Schulenburg/The Interior Archive, 87

Andrew Wood /The Interior Archive, 55 (bottom); 122 (top)

©Homes & Ideas/Andrew Cameron /IPC Media Ltd., 36

©Homes & Ideas/ Spike Powell/IPC Media Ltd., 42 (top); 75; 134 (bottom)

©Homes & Ideas/Lucinda Symons/IPC Media Ltd., 33 (top); 137 (top)

©Homes & Ideas/Simon Whitmore /IPC Media Ltd., 18

©Houses & Interiors/Steve Hawkins/Teresa Ward, 83

©Living, Etc./Craig Knowles/IPC Media Ltd., 51 (top)

©Living, Etc./Ed Reeve/IPC Syndication, 12 (middle); 32 (bottom)

©Living Etc./Polly Wreford/IPC Media Ltd., 61

©Living Etc./Tim Young/IPC Media Ltd., 17

Greg Premru, 105; 138 (bottom)

ABOUT THE AUTHOR

Sarah Lynch is an editor on staff at *Metropolitan Home*. For each issue she writes a column called "Colorways" that gives advice and information about one chosen color. Her favorite color is pink! She lives in Park Slope, Brooklyn.

Acknowledgments

I would like to thank Debbie Needleman for her tireless photo research and support, without which this project never would have made it. Additional thanks go to my editor, Shawna Mullen, for her calming nature which helped me down off the ledge more than once.

This book is dedicated to Ben and Heather, whose daily support and patience did not go unnoticed. And to my mother for passing down an appreciation of bold colors.